P9-DXH-736

DATE DUE

DE 18 '03			

DEMCO 38-296

ETHICS

WITHOUT

GOD

REVISED EDITION

ETHICS WITHOUT GOD

REVISED EDITION

KAI NIELSEN

PROMETHEUS BOOKS • BUFFALO, NEW YORK

Riverside Community College /
Library
4800 Magnolia Avenue
Riverside, California 92506

BJ1012 .N53 1990
Nielsen, Kai, 1926–
Ethics without God

Published 1990 by Prometheus Books
700 East Amherst Street, Buffalo, New York 14215

Copyright © 1990 by Kai Nielsen
All Rights Reserved

No part of this book may be reproduced or transmitted in any form or by
any means without prior permission in writing from the publisher, except
by a reviewer who wishes to quote brief passages for inclusion in a maga
zine, newspaper, or broadcast.

Library of Congress Cataloging-in-Publication Data

Nielsen, Kai, 1926–
    Ethics Without God/by Kai Nielsen.
        p.   cm.
    Includes bibliographical references.
    ISBN 0-87975-552-0
    1. Ethics. 2. Religious ethics—Controversial literature.
3. Natural law—Controversial literature. I. Title.
BJ1012.N53   1989
171',1dc20   89-3972
                                                                 CIP

Printed in the United States of America

To

Stanley Stein

Contents

Preface

This revised edition of my *Ethics Without God,* originally published in 1972, is a considerably expanded edition. Five new chapters have been added. I felt a principal weakness of the first edition was that it contained no discussion of the natural law tradition or of the sociological functions of religion, functions that might be thought necessary for social solidarity or full human flourishing. Chapter 1 remedies that by an extensive discussion of both issues. There is also added a discussion of immorality vis-à-vis mortality and an expanded and nuanced discussion of the Divine Command theory, including responses to some critiques of the first addition of my book. Finally, I have discussed alternatives within secular ethics and, in the final chapter, I have given a capsule account of my own secular account of ethics more extensively developed in my *Equality and Liberty, Marxism and the Moral Point of View,* and *Why Be Moral?*

Kai Nielsen,
Calgary, Alberta,
Canada
September 1989

1

On Keeping the Wolf at Bay

I

Robert Bellah has noted that Americans have a kind of civil religion, an undifferentiated theism, that all American presidents from Washington to Reagan trot out on significant public occasions as the basis for the moral viability of American society and to justify what many Americans take to be America's mission in the world.[1] In specific presidential and other official articulations, where this civil religion is most in evidence, there is an avoidance of any sectarian formulations appealing specifically to any denomination of Christianity or even to Christianity generally. Christ is not talked about, but rather God and the natural moral law that He has promulgated for His creation. His providential ordering of things plays a considerable role during public occasions such as state of the union addresses and the like. This is a very deeply ingrained feature in the typical American's consciousness. It is, if you will, a central feature of the American moral ideology.

My concern here is not with the sociological accuracy of this claim, but with whether or not this moral ideology (if that is the right phrase for it) is a distorting and groundless conception. I want to know whether the American social fabric, or any social fabric, would be undermined if that religiosity were lost and not replaced by a closely related religious belief system.

9

There is an ambiguity in that question to which I should first attend. If America lost its civil religion, it would have a different social fabric than it now has. But this trivial truth is not what people are concerned with when they worry that if belief in a transcendent God disintegrates, then morality and democracy will be destroyed. It is, understandably, not some small change in the social fabric that worries them but whether if God is dead, nothing matters. If people come to reject a belief in God, will they become beings without a moral sense who are simply trained animals? The worry is that without belief in God there is no rhyme or reason to morality; that moral commitment, including commitments to human rights and democracy, will be destroyed. I am, of course, aware that many people believe such things and indeed that many who do not exactly harbor these beliefs fear that something like them might be so. I try to show in this volume that their fears are groundless.[2] God or no God, the torturing of innocents is evil; God or no God, wife beating or child molesting is vile. More generally, even if we can make nothing of the concept of God, we can readily come to appreciate, if we would but reflect and take the matter to heart, that, if anything is evil, inflicting or tolerating unnecessary and pointless suffering is evil, especially when something can be done about it. If that isn't evil, I ask, what is evil? Can't we be more confident about this than we can about any abstract or general philosophical point we might make in ethical theory?

However, all that notwithstanding, it will be responded that I said "If anything is evil." But how do I show, or know, that anything is evil? To cut immediately to the quick and to concede for the nonce more than I would in reality be prepared to, perhaps we cannot demonstrate or in any way prove that anything is evil. But we can say, quite unequivocally, that it is more reasonable to believe such elemental things to be evil than to believe either any skeptical theory that tells us we cannot know or even reasonably believe any of these things to be evil, or to believe some philosophical or theological theory that tells us we can *only justifiably* believe these things to be evil by coming to know God and His eternal moral law for humankind.[3]

I firmly believe that this is bedrock and right and that anyone who does not believe it cannot have probed deeply enough into the grounds of his moral beliefs. Some, at least, will think that this is too short a way with dissenters, and there certainly are a number of objections and alternatives that readily spring to mind. I will now consider them.

II

I will attempt three things here. First, I shall criticize a kind of causal argument that would accept my earlier claim and still argue that I fail with this abstract and general claim to touch base, as current slang has it, with the realities of our human life. (I shall explain that dark saying in a moment.) Second, I shall gesture at a reasonable basis for moral belief that is utterly secular, and, third, I shall criticize a standard religious foundation for morality that I did not criticize in the first edition of *Ethics Without God,* namely, the doctrine, particularly popular in Catholic and Anglican circles, though not limited to those circles, that the basis of morality is in what is called the natural moral law, a doctrine that might, not implausibly, be thought to underlie the civil religion of America and more than a few other societies.

Let me turn to my first point and to an explanation of my dark saying. I said that we can know that some things are evil—say the torturing of innocent children just for the fun of it—completely independently of belief in God or even having any understanding of the concept of God. Some will concede this. They will agree, that is, that God or no God, such things can be known or at least reasonably and quite unequivocally held to be wrong. It is not here, some will say, that we need belief in God vis-à-vis moral belief but as a *causal mechanism* to keep the wolf in us all at bay. Emile Durkheim and Max Weber, thorough secularists that they were, have shown us, though in somewhat different ways, the fundamental role that religion plays in stabilizing society. Rational or irrational/non-rational, coherent or incoherent, religious belief—as long as it is not seen or felt to be irrational or incoherent or otherwise groundless—has a stabilizing effect in society. Where, in the dreadful life of the ghetto, Blacks can maintain their religion, they are much less likely to be destroyed by drugs and the like.

Belief in God, which is an essential part of religious belief in
our culture, though not in all cultures, is an essential stabilizing
device for us as a people, keeping Tootle straight on the tracks
no matter what. Without such social bonding, people, or at least
most people, will feel alienated and disaffected from their society.
Their lives will become meaningless and without direction.

This mild causal attribution gets a far more extremist
articulation by people like Paul Johnson.[4] The roots of the horror
of the twentieth century, he tells us, lie in the breakdown of
an absolutistic Christian morality, a morality that functions
as the kind of social mechanism I have been talking about.
Much of the evil in our world, he assures us, is the direct result
of the decline of Christianity. Without religion we would scarcely
be human beings. Without God, he declaims, men quickly become subhuman, veritable Jekyll and Hyde creatures. Moreover, state power is not sufficient to keep the masses in check.
We need, in addition, Christianity as a form of social control.
Without it we will have something like the state of nature in
which life is nasty, brutish, and short.

These are rather large-scale and grand causal attributions
about how people behave and how societies must sustain
themselves if they are to be even tolerably humane. For such
strong claims and for claims of such scope we need very good
evidence indeed. The evidence that Johnson provides, rooted
in a particular historical narrative he gives us, goes something
like this. The Western world order had its origins in Christianity.
This worked, with its ups and downs, reasonably well, throughout the nineteenth century, even with all its theological turmoil.
The turning point was 1914 with the commencement of the
First World War. That, among other things, drained our moral
energies and engendered cynicism and a distrust of Christianity.
Two powerful, charismatic, vehemently Godless, and religion-
abominating ideologies arose out of this moral vacuum, to wit
Bolshevism and Nazism, both with their charismatic leaders
and both dedicated to eradicating Christian values. The atheistic
world that emerged was a horror.

Johnson, echoing things said before him by, among others,
T. S. Eliot, quickly concludes that we cannot have a Godless
world. What we need instead is Christianity (not just religion)
as a method of social control. (He does not speak about the truth

or validity of its claims.) We must, the claim goes, be so socialized that each of us will believe that we are accountable for our actions to some ultimate tribunal whose proclamations are unquestionable. There can be no such thing as liberal choice here.

Christianity cannot perfect human beings. The perfection of man is a liberal and Marxist fairytale. But it can control the wolf in us. Christianity cannot perfect man but it can make us better than we would otherwise be, and it can do this in a way no Godless creed or any other religion can. Some of us may be able to recognize certain things to be right or wrong without belief in God, but society will not be well-ordered—indeed, it will be barbaric—without Christianity as a method of social control.

III

There are two things I want to say here. First, this is a very selective and interpretive historical thesis and there are a number of rival interpretations that take into account the same range of evidence. The high Nazi leaders and Nazi intelligentsia were anti-Christian but anti-Semitism was deeply rooted in German and Austrian societies, which were pervasively Christian societies, and in Polish and Hungarian societies, both of which were deeply Christian. (Secular Denmark was another kettle of fish.) Catholics and Protestants were among those staffing the concentration camps. Some clergymen were indeed exemplary but the church as a whole did not oppose Hitler, and to the end, Germany under Hitler remained both loyal to the Führer *and* Christian. A not inconsiderable number of the German intelligentsia, both Jewish and non-Jewish, left Germany and many who did so were thoroughly secular. To attribute the barbaric quality of Nazism to the breakdown of Christianity is at best unrealistic. It attributes far too much causal power to the beliefs of a few intellectuals.

The story is somewhat different with the Soviet Union. There what is most crucial to recognize is that we had an ill-educated society of impoverished peasants who were closely bound to Holy Mother Church and who had no understanding of anything other than autocratic rule. It was a society where secularization had only touched a few intelligentsia, a minuscule part of the population. To attribute the ills of Russian society to the claim that it is a secularized society is at best naive.

To support the we-need-Christianity-to-keep-the-wolf-at-bay hypothesis, we need to involve a tendentious and, I believe, mistaken reading of the historical record. But, more importantly, there is disconfirming evidence for this hypothesis, which it fails to meet in anything like an adequate way. Indeed, in the face of such evidence, it deploys additional *ad hoc* and implausible hypotheses.

In an effort to uncover this disconfirming evidence, first consider Japan and then consider the Scandinavian countries, from Iceland on the west to Finland on the east. Post World War II Japan is surely a non-Christian society; yet it is a stable one, a not inhumane one (as societies go), and at least by conventional Western standards a flourishing capitalist democracy. To say that this is a result of the Christianizing influence of the brief American occupation of Japan after the war surely (*a*) attributes too strong an effect to that influence and (*b*) does not explain why it so sustains itself without ever having become or even having tended to become a Christian society. The Scandinavian countries (all of them) are the strongest disconfirming evidence to the we-need-Christianity-to-keep-the-wolf-at-bay hypothesis. They are among the most highly educated, affluent, and the most secularized societies we have today, yet they are all without exception, flourishing, open societies with firm, valid democratic traditions. Moreover, they are stable societies that are prospering economically with high standards of living (by capitalist standards at least) that extensively trickle down to most of their members. They are among the most egalitarian societies in the world and some of the freest. Yet these, let me repeat, are deeply secularized societies where religion is steadily, but untraumatically, losing its grip. To say, by way of response, as Johnson does, that Sweden is an oppressive, quasi-totalitarian society is pure fantasy. Swedes are perfectly free to emigrate. There is no Swedish Curtain, and with their high level of education (generally speaking) and mastery of languages it would be easy for many of them to emigrate. But few do.

The second thing I want to say about the we-need-Christianity-to-keep-the-wolf-at-bay hypothesis is that it is not as philosophically innocent and purely historical as Johnson gives us to understand. It is a very philosophically slanted historical thesis and the philosophy in it is unargued and appears to be groundless. He says that without religion we would scarcely be human beings: without God man quickly becomes subhuman. *How* does he know this, or *does* he know it? I have already queried his historical evidence as a generalization about most men in all societies. Perhaps he has some psychological evidence for it. But he gives us none, and in the face of the counter-evidence it would have to be very good indeed. Given the state of psychology as a science, this is very unlikely. There are plenty of atheists and agnostics around who are persons of integrity, moral compassion, understanding, and sensitivity. Johnson, I have been given to understand, knew Bertrand Russell and Hugh Gaitskell well. Could he have seriously wondered, if even for a moment, that they were moral monsters who were scarcely human? There have been atheists who were clearly bad sorts—Stalin, for example—but the same could be said for some Christians—Loyola, Franco, and Salazar for starters. (Don't say they are not real Christians. That would be playing with words. Atheists could play that game, too.) But among the famous skeptical intelligentsia there are many who are among our examples of moral integrity, compassion, understanding, and decency. Can it with any plausibility at all be said that Lucretius, Spinoza, J. S. Mill, Hume, George Eliot, Gottfried Keller, Albert Einstein, George Bernard Shaw, John Dewey, Erich Fromm, Edward Westermarck, Axel Hägerström, or Bertrand Russell were scarcely human? To even raise the question is to see how absurd the claim is. It is simply an utterly false and groundless dogma to claim that without religion people would be scarcely human. If you think that you personally would also be scarcely human if you lost faith, think again. If you have a child, would you simply start socking the youngster around if you lost your faith or would you stop loving your child or have reason to stop loving your child? Would losing your faith make any difference at all in these matters? If you say, I believe incongruously, yes, ask yourself, "Should it?" Do you only love your child because God commands it or because God exists? I submit that you don't *only* love your child for these reasons, and you shouldn't. *Perhaps* we have even more reason to love each other if there is no God for then the only thing we have is each other.

Be that as it may, there is *no* reason at all to believe that if we don't believe in God, we would be scarcely human, but every good reason to believe that the claim is false.

IV

However, the we-need-religion-to-keep-the-wolf-at-bay hypothesis is a rather extravagant one. Let me return now to the weaker and much more plausible Weberian and Durkheimian proposition from which we started, namely, the contention that religion has a vital social role in stabilizing society. I will pass over the point that on some occasions it might be a very good thing indeed if some societies would be destabilized. Instead, I will consider not only what is manifestly true, namely, that religion has played a vital role in stabilizing society so that a decent social fabric remains intact, but also whether religion is *necessary* for a stable society such that if through secularization religion withered away, would society be so destabilized that it would lose any kind of decent social fabric? That is an empirical possibility, particularly in societies where the religion had been very authoritarian and the secularization was forced. But I think it very unlikely for at least three reasons, one a rather straightforward empirical reason and the other two theoretical.

First the empirical point: Let us consider the Scandinavian countries again. Here, as I have already remarked, secularization has dug deeper than anywhere else in the world but the moral fabric of these societies has remained intact or at least, if we get very normative, they are as intact as is the morality of any of the more religiously oriented industrial societies. The scheduling of values has in certain respects changed, though one must not exaggerate that, but the moral fabric has remained. These societies are more egalitarian and less sexist than they were; they are even freer than they were in the past. Respect for civil liberties, for example, is fully in place. There remains, at least as much as in the more Christian or Jewish or Islamic societies, moral integrity, a sense of individual responsibility, compassion, and respect for individual rights.

I have heard it said of Sweden by some conservative Christians that it has lost its values. All this could sensibly mean is either that it has lost certain distinctively Judeo-Christian values—not that it has lost the very central values mentioned above, those shared not only by Christians but by almost everyone else as well in Westernized societies—or, less interestingly, that Swedes have lost certain values that were appropriate to peasant society. There is, I suspect, some loss there but there is also a gain as well and it is a debatable question whether on balance the gain is not greater than the loss. But in any event, a movement away from peasant society is unavoidable (empirically speaking, inevitable) with the development of the productive forces. There is no turning back from this. However, the central thing to see here is that even if there are some alterations in values in Sweden, there is no good reason to think that its morality is undermined. Central, widely shared values remain perfectly in place.

I want now to turn to my theoretical reasons for thinking that the moral fabric of society would not be rent by Godlessness. What makes us moral beings is not so much the theoretical belief systems we inherit, religious or secular, but the way we have been nurtured from very early on. If we were fortunate enough to have had good moral role models, that is, kind, tolerably wise, and understanding parents, and to have lived in conditions of security where our basic needs were stably met, the chances are reasonably good that we will have those desirable moral characteristics ourselves. Our very basic moral character is importantly structured by those things. Secular beliefs, or for that matter religious beliefs, are not going to undermine these *psychological* foundations of moral belief. Suppose that you grew up in such a well-knit religious family and in your adulthood or near adulthood there comes a time when you no longer believe in God but yet these secure psychological moral foundations remain intact. There is every reason to believe that you will pass on to your children, though without certain inessential religious elaborations, these central moral values and that they will pass them on to their children and so on. There is good reason to think, if the moral beliefs have a rationale, that they will remain, and if they do not have a rationale, that they will still remain as mere psychologically reinforced habits.

I now wish to turn to my second theoretical consideration.

I showed with swift strokes—perhaps too swiftly—at the very beginning that even in a Godless world we would have good reason not to torture the innocent, not to be cruel to our children, not to betray our friends, and the like. There are many reasons for not doing such things, and none of them have anything to do with belief in God. Perhaps the most bedrock one is that we both care about our fellow human beings and about ourselves, and that we do not want to do these things or have them happen to ourselves or others. If someone asks, "Why care about ourselves and others?" perhaps the most honest answer is to say that we just do and turn the question back on our interlocutor and ask him if he has a better reason for not doing these things. If he responds that the better reason is that it is against God's law, then we can ask, playing this absurd game, "Why care about God's law?" He may say "Well I just do." And he is back once again to caring, a caring that, like a wheel that turns no machinery, just adds another caring to our original shared carings.

Suppose he says, alternatively, "I care about God's law because otherwise I am afraid I might fry in hell for eternity." But that is hardly a very commendable moral reason for caring about people or for refraining from doing certain things. Could we honestly, in our heart of hearts, think highly of a person whose *only* reason for not beating up on his child is that he is afraid that if he does he will go to hell?

It may well be true that I and other atheists like me only *came* to have our moral beliefs because of certain things in a Christian, Jewish, or Islamic tradition, certain beliefs and habits that were handed on to us from one or another of those traditions. But we must beware of committing the genetic fallacy. The validity of a belief is independent of its origin. That Stalin said something is not in and of itself sufficient to make it false. Whether we are justified in believing it to be true or false depends on the evidence. That Reagan said the same thing doesn't make it true, for exactly the same reason. How I got my beliefs is one thing. Whether I am justified in believing them is another. And, no matter what their origin, if I have good grounds for believing what I do, I am, *ceteris paribus* (all things being equal), justified in so believing. What justifies my belief that I must not break trust with my friends is not how I happened to come to that belief but what grounds I can give for it. That I got my values from my Christian upbringing, even if that is true, is not what justifies my values. What justifies them is many things, including that I care about my friends, about myself, and about what sort of person I am. Further reasons are the fact that the breaking of trust not only destroys social relations and thus harms society but causes suffering as well. All of these are perfectly good reasons whether or not there is a God or people to believe in Him, and belief in God could not be a better reason for not breaking trust with your friends than the reasons I have just given.

V

I think someone could come to agree with what I have argued above and still wish for something more objective than those carings, albeit reflective carings, to which I have appealed. In my more *philosophically* skeptical moments I think there is nothing more objective to which we can appeal. What I have, in effect, argued in the previous sections, is that, humanly speaking, if that is all the objectivity we can get, that is quite enough. But I expect we can get a little something more in the way of objectivity. I want to pursue this a bit here.

There is to my mind a very hopeful way of proceeding, a way applied to ethics by John Rawls from epistemological procedures developed in other contexts by Nelson Goodman and V. W. O. Quine and extended by other moral philosophers who are close to Rawls in their outlook.[5] This method, if that is the right word for it, has been given the rather unattractive title of an *appeal to considered judgments in wide reflective equilibrium.* Let me explain what this means. We start with firmly fixed considered moral judgments such as the ones I mentioned at the outset. (Other salient ones would be the belief that religious or racial intolerance is unacceptable, that promises must not be lightly broken, that we need to have a regard for the truth, that people are never to be treated as means only, and the like.) Starting with those considered moral convictions that we hold most firmly, we see whether we can arrange them into a coherent and, of course, consistent package. We should also take the extant moral theories and see how well they match with these considered judgments. The relation is much like that of scientific theories to observed experimental data. If we have two scientific theories, A and B, and A accounts for more of the data than B, then, *ceteris paribus,* we should accept theory A rather than B.

Exactly similar things obtain for moral theories. The theory that squares best with and explains best this consistent set of confidently held considered judgments is, *ceteris paribus,* the theory we should accept. *Ceteris,* however, may not be *paribus.* The theories themselves must also have intrinsic plausibility. They must be reasonably well defined (clearly stated) and they must have no incoherent conceptions. If some of their conceptualizations—some of which may be more abstract considered judgments themselves—are more problematic than those of an alternative theory that does not make quite as tight a fit with the set of less theoretical considered judgments as does the theory with the more problematic conceptualizations, then it is not clear which theory is preferable. However, if the theory that has the more problematic conceptualizations but accounts for more data could be clarified so that the problematic conceptualizations were no longer problematic, then it, in virtue of the fact that it accounts for more of these firmly fixed considered judgments, would be the clear winner.

However, it is not just a matter of getting as coherent a fit as possible between considered judgments and moral theory; we also use the moral theory together with this set of considered judgments to assess moral convictions of which we are less sure. We all have moral conceptions that are, for us, half-convictions, of which we are ambivalent or at least not entirely sure. I am inclined to think that under many circumstances euthanasia is justified, but I am not sure. If, on careful inspection, I find that when employed with safeguards, euthanasia squares with my other considered judgments, the moral theory that best explains them, and with what is known about the facts, then I have been given a very good reason to firm up my wavering judgment about euthanasia. If it goes the other way, I have been given good reason to reject or at least modify my judgment. In this way moral theories and, more generally, the method of wide reflective equilibrium, can criticize and correct moral judgments. Moreover, the method of *wide* reflective equilibrium is not, like an intuitionist system, simply a matter of getting a coherent set. We have a basis for rejecting or accepting moral claims of which we are less certain or for coming to state and accept new moral claims that might be generated from the theory, from what we know about the world, and from the consistent set of considered moral judgments.

I mentioned above the importance of squaring our moral judgments with what is known about the world. (This says nothing about deriving an ought from an is.)[6] However, that in effect introduced a new element. *Wide* reflective equilibrium must not only seek the most coherent fit possible between considered judgments and moral theories, it must also seek the most coherent fit between considered judgments; moral theories; the most accurate account available to us of the nonmoral facts (if that is not pleonastic); and the best social, scientific, and philosophical theories we have. We shuttle back and forth adjusting sometimes our considered judgments or sometimes our moral theories until we get the most coherent representation compatible with what we know about the world, including what we know about human nature and society. In this attempt to get such a coherent picture, we need to recognize that not even our most firm considered judgments are *in principle* immune from revision or rejection. But this does not give us the slightest reason to think that they will ever be rejected or revised in any extensive way. It only shows us that we have a fallibilistic (not a skeptical) world view and that we are not going to get certainty. But in science and other factual domains we have learned to live quite comfortably without certainty. We can have knowledge and objectivity without certainty. ("Certain knowledge" is not a redundancy.) There is no reason to think that in the realm of morality we cannot in a similar way come of age and live without absolute certainty.

This account has been criticized on the grounds that it is disanalogous with science. Quite apart from any pattern of coherence in reflective equilibrium, the observation reports of a scientific theory have *some* antecedent credibility. This is not true of considered judgments. There is no way of directly (or perhaps indirectly) verifying them or, independent of adopting some contestable theory, showing them to be true. The observation reports are by contrast verifiable and can be shown to be true independently of adopting some theory.

I agree that at least some considered judgments cannot be verified and I do not want to give them the same logical status as observation reports. Where does this lead one? If what I have said is near to the mark, then very fundamental moral and value judgments, some of them firmly fixed considered judgments, are not judgments that can be verified. It seems to me that Henry Sidgwick was right in arguing that all we can do is carefully reflect on them and see how they fit into coherent patterns. When coherence is established and still someone presses for a reason to accept our most firmly fixed judgments—we could at least as far as logical possibilities are concerned, have had other starting points, other considered judgments—all we can finally do, for those judgments that are not dependent on factual claims, is to say that we have reflected carefully on them, taken the matter to heart, and when we do these are the judgments to which we feel committed. The rationalist hopes to get behind these judgments to something more objective, but his attempts have always failed. The history of moral philosophy shows how deeply they come a cropper here. You can, if it makes you feel better, say you have intuited a synthetic *a priori* truth or have become aware of some ontologically esoteric fact/value. But this is mere arm-waving. It explains nothing and, as Bertrand Russell pointed out, it only gives the illusion of greater objectivity.[7]

This would be unsettling indeed if there were not a very considerable *de facto* consensus quite world wide. People will dispute about just who are innocent and who are not, but, all the same, there will be no society in which people take it to be tolerable that innocent children can be tortured just for the fun of it or that friends can break trust easily or treat their promises lightly or randomly kill people on a whim. These are all obvious things but they do show, whatever their logical status, that there is a wide cross-cultural consensus about such actions. When we can also show, that these considered judgments are not in conflict with anything we factually know or have good grounds for believing then their acceptability is further enhanced. Where this is so we do not have to rely on a brute *de facto consensus*.

It could be that people would start with quite different and incompatible considered judgments and make different wide reflective equilibria. If that obtained, there would be no way to prove one equilibrium to be more reasonable than another. But, fortunately, we do not in fact have these radically different equilibria, like we have radically different geometries. We do indeed have different considered judgments but we also have shared considered judgments, and when these judgments are also shown to stand in wide reflective equilibrium, this gives us a reasonable measure of objectivity. When we work it out we come to see that we do share considered judgments in a wide reflective equilibrium. Things might have been different, but in fact they are not.

It is also the case that the method of wide reflective equilibrium can give us a rational procedure for arguing about considered judgments. The considered judgments of many Christians would conflict with considered judgments of many, if not most, secularists. Many Christians believe that under all circumstances suicide is wrong, abortion is wrong, and pre-marital intercourse is wrong. It is clear enough, if a reflective discussion of the matter is permitted to proceed, that many Christians would grant that if there were no God to forbid it, suicide under certain circumstances would not only be permissible but admirable. They believe in a God who categorically forbids suicide and that we must not, no matter what the circumstances, do that which God forbids. According to some Christians, God categorically forbids suicide and so they conclude that suicide is wrong. But if we use the method of wide reflective equilibrium, we also know that we must get our moral judgments in such an equilibrium. But this means that we must square them with what we know. There are serious and deep questions about whether the concept of God is a coherent concept and, beyond that, even if we can make sense of the concept, there is still the problem of whether there are good reasons for believing that there is a God or whether belief in God is rationally justified.

Where we are using the method of wide reflective equilibrium, these are questions that cannot be bypassed when appealing to such considered judgments. If the believer takes a Fideist turn and says he simply accepts God's word on faith, then vis-à-vis those moral judgments of his that conflict with the secularist, there is still a very real question, that the method of wide reflective equilibrium will not let him bypass. He must face the fact that there are many faiths and there are many putative revelations, which sometimes conflict (and on occasion radically). They also sometimes have significantly different conceptions about how people are to live their lives. What we must do, if we are to follow the method of wide reflective equilibrium, is to see how these various faiths square with the other things we know and with extant moral theories and conceptions. If we are reasonable, we cannot just plunk—make an arbitrary Kierkegaardean leap of faith—for one of these faiths. (Even if we think wide reflective equilibrium makes too strong of a demand, we cannot jump in like this.) The short of it is that the religious believer, in making such distinctively religious moral judgments, is not travelling ontologically light. He ties moral beliefs to definite cosmological claims and, if he is not to be arbitrary, he must indicate how these cosmological claims can be justified.

This is particularly evident if he would use the method of wide reflective equilibrium, which appears at least to be the only game in town that will enable us to show how moral claims can be justified. It could be said that the method simply puts our various claims before the bar of reason. We attempt to show how all these beliefs go together into a coherent whole that best squares with what we have observed to be the case and to what, on deepest moral reflection, we would continue to commit ourselves, knowing that, since we are human beings, we start with a battery of moral convictions. But so treated these considered convictions are no longer helter skelter. Instead, they fit together with what we can reasonably believe or at least reasonably hope. When people speak of living the life of reason or being committed to reason it seems to me that this is what they mean or at least what they should mean.

There have been philosophers on the quest for certainty who have wanted a more substantive and less procedural conception of reasonability. Some of them might very well say that, with my appeal to considered judgments and with the use I make of it, I show that I am really appealing, albeit unwittingly, to the natural moral law, though, unfortunately, I do not carry through on this and come to accept the secure rational foundations for the natural moral law given in Thomism.

In the next section, after expounding such a standard conception of the natural moral law, I will try to show that these natural law foundations are actually in shambles and, in a later section, I shall argue that it is a mistake even to appeal, in talking of such fundamental considered convictions, to a demythologized version of the natural moral law.

VI

Cardinal Mercier (a distinguished neo-Thomist) argues, as does St. Thomas Aquinas himself, that the ultimate grounds for the moral law must be found in God, for there can be no law without a lawgiver and where moral laws are concerned, God alone has the *power* and *right* to issue commands to his subjects.[8] On this point of Mercier's, there is an extensive agreement among Jewish and Christian moralists.

But Mercier, and the natural moral law tradition that he represents, breaks with some fellow religionists when the additional claim is made that we humans do have some *natural* knowledge of good and evil. We are all sinners, he believes; there is, indeed, corruption in the palace of justice for we are all infected with the sin of Adam; but that notwithstanding, we still have a natural capacity to distinguish good from evil. All persons, have within themselves, some natural knowledge of good and evil. In some it is undeveloped; some hardly exercise it at all, but quite apart from any Divine revelation they may or may not have had, they have some rudimentary knowledge of how they ought to behave. Contrary to Emile Brunner, we do not need a positive revelation from God to discern the difference between good and evil.[9] Moral obligations, as Aquinas has argued, rest on "a double foundation—immediately upon human nature; remotely upon the intelligence of God who rules all things by his Providence."[10]

There is a further point that distinguishes this natural law position from that of a Protestant religious moralist such as Brunner. The ultimate source of God's goodness—for Aquinas, for Mercier, and for neo-Thomists generally—is not in God's will, but in His reason.[11] God alone knows His own essence; He alone knows Himself as a necessary good. God perceives that He is good and issues commands and injunctions according to His own insight into His essential goodness. Something doesn't become good simply because God commands it; the goodness of the thing is, we are told, in God's very nature.

The natural moral laws emanating from God are not simply divine fiats; they are the ordinances of His reason. They are proclaimed by God for the good of man. All human beings, unless utterly perverted by sin, have those natural inclinations, which dispose them to *know* these moral laws of God. God has given us an intellectual tendency to form some principles of reason with certainty. We have the ability to apprehend some objective moral truths. We can do this if we will only carefully and nonevasively reflect on our own nature. Like Aristotle, Mercier and the Thomistic natural law tradition generally, argue that the good of a thing "is what answers to its natural tendency," and thus "the moral good is that which answers to the tendency of the rational nature of man. . . ."[12] If we will only with great care and nonevasiveness reflect on the end or purpose of our own rational natures as human beings, we will come to understand that the fundamental purpose of our existence is to love God and to try to be like Him. Without this purpose, without this overall rationale, our lives as human beings will remain pointless and senseless. We will be forced, as Pascal observed, to load our lives with distractions because we will not be able to bear to be alone with ourselves; we will not be able to bear our pointless, senseless existence. Where a human being cannot distract himself, he will suffer despair or debilitating anxiety—as Kierkegaard put it, "sickness unto death"—for his life will have no *ultimate goal.*

Man, in the moral domain, has one overriding, absolutely true, self-evident principle, the truth of which he immediately apprehends. That first principle is simply this: *good is to be done and evil is to be avoided.* No one, who thinks clearly about what he is doing can doubt this for a second. He is immediately and directly aware of its truth.

This by itself, however, is not enough for it does not tell us *what* is good. But there are other natural moral laws that do tell human beings what they ought to do. Aquinas and the neo-Thomists who followed him would have us believe that these principles are certain and that they do give content to the natural moral law. But the content is to a degree indeterminate. Natural moral law theorists, where they have been wise, have not attempted to give an exhaustive list of natural laws. The following are typical examples:

1) Life ought to be preserved.

2) Man ought to propagate his kind.

3) Children ought to be educated.

4) Property rights ought to be respected.

5) Ignorance ought to be avoided.

6) Man ought to know the truth about God.

They are, as Cardinal Mercier puts it, "the invincible convictions of the human race."[13] Our *intellect* apprehends these laws as good. They are cross-culturally valid. All men, everywhere, have held them. They are, in another of Cardinal Mercier's phrases, "the compelling truths which are anterior to every code of merely human origin and independent of all contingent circumstances."[14] The distinction between good and evil does not lie in ancient custom but "is founded on the very nature of things."

God, Aquinas and the Thomists argue, is the *extrinsic* principle moving human beings to be good; and God instructs us by means of His law. But what is this law that we are to follow? What is the *essence* of law? Is the law something pertaining to reason? Aquinas answers that it is. Law is not merely any arbitrary fiat that pleases the sovereign. "Law," Aquinas tells us, "is a rule and measure of acts, whereby man is induced to act or is restrained from acting. . . ."[15] But it belongs to reason to command, and reason is the rule and measure of human acts. Thus, since law is a rule and measure of acts, reason pertains to law.

Yet have Aquinas and Mercier done anything here but give us a set of stipulative definitions? *If* we accept such definitions, what they say may well follow, but why should we accept these definitions? There can be and indeed are irrational commands and rules. Perhaps—because of some moral convictions or some considered judgments of our own—we want it to be the case that rules and commands are not merely the whims of some sovereign, some Caligula in command, but how are we to establish that only commands and rules that are reasonable are those that constitute laws? They indeed may be the only *good* rules or *good* laws, but this is a different matter. And how does Aquinas know—or does he know—that the rule and measure of human acts is reason? No doubt it *should* be, but assuming that law *should* be rational, how do we know that the rule of human action is in fact reason rather than custom or merely a blind preference? Is it not more likely that the rule is sometimes one of these things and sometimes another? As far as I can see, Aquinas has simply asked us to accept certain stipulative *definitions* that would rule out the possibility of there being a law that was merely a sovereign fiat. He has given us no reason to believe that his definition somehow *encapsulates* what is antecedently recognized as law. In short, Aquinas does not show that law is something that must be in accord with reason. Indeed, it is not even clear that such a conception has a reading that is both interesting and intelligible.

In order "that the volition of what is commanded may have the nature of law," Aquinas tells us, "it needs to be in accord with some rule of reason."[16] This indeed corresponds to something that we would all like to be true, but have we any reason at all to think that it is? Consider the decisions of the American or Canadian Supreme Court, for example. Are they all rules of reason? If, on the one hand, we say they are, are we not playing fast and loose with the meaning of 'rules of reason'? On the other hand, if we say that those with which we are not in accord are not laws, then are we playing fast and loose with the meaning of 'law'. It seems to me that the Thomist is trapped here whichever way he goes.

Aquinas also argues that law is directed to the common good. If Aquinas's argument is to get going, we must accept what we have just rejected, namely, that law of necessity pertains to reason. Reason, as a principle of human acts, is, according to Aquinas, the principle that governs all the rest. Law, he claims, must be referred to this. Now, where questions of human conduct are concerned, the first principle of action— the *end* for which all other actions concerning how to live are undertaken—is *happiness* or *beatitude.* "Consequently, law must needs concern itself mainly with the order that is in beatitude."[17] Since no man is an island, since each individual is ordained to be a part of the main, without which his distinctive human qualities cannot be realized, "law must needs concern itself properly with the order directed to universal happiness."[18] That is to say, law is ordained to produce happiness in the body politic. Thus every law, on such a conception, is ordained for the common good.

Let us now assume for the sake of the argument that Aquinas has established that for a law to be a law it must be a rule of reason. Let us now see if he can show that every law is ordained for the common good. How do we know that there is one thing—happiness, beatitude, or whatnot—that is the *rationale* of all rules of reason? Perhaps there are many. Why assume that the *only* ultimate or overriding end in life is human happiness? Even if there is only one such end, how do we know it is happiness or beatitude? Man is indeed a social animal: he can only live a meaningful life in society, but *why* must an individual always act, to be acting *rationally,* for the good of that social order? It is indeed true, as Hobbes shows, that if people generally do not consider the interests of others—if no man curbs his egoistic drives—they will indeed find themselves in a state of nature in which life is nasty, brutish, and short. But an *individual* in a settled social situation could act immorally without radically upsetting the social order. Free-riders sometimes flourish. Why couldn't a man act rationally and still not act for the common good? (That *morally speaking* he *ought* to act for the common good is another question.) At best Aquinas has established that all law *ought* to be for the common good, but not that all law, in order to be law, *is* for or directed to the common good. Even here we should say that no law *ought* to be against the common good, not that all law is for the common good. When I enter into a contract, get married, or make a will, I need not be doing anything for the common good. Yet what I do is, and no doubt should be, legally binding.

Aquinas, in the context of trying to show how a law to be a law must be promulgated, gives us his definition of 'law'. "Law is nothing else than an ordinance of reason for the common good, promulgated by him who has the care of the community."[19] The natural law, which is written in the hearts of human beings, is promulgated "by the very fact that God instilled it into man's mind so as to be known by him naturally."[20]

It is at this point in his "Treatise on Law," that Aquinas considers the various kinds of law. He thinks there is *eternal* law, *natural* law, *human* law, and *divine* law. *Natural* law, for Aquinas, is part of the *eternal* law. Eternal law "is nothing else than the exemplar of divine wisdom, as directing all actions and movements."[21] It is God's blueprint for man. *The natural law is that part of the eternal law man can know apart from revelation.*

How, we should ask at this point, do we know there is an *eternal* law? Aquinas answers that if it is granted that the world is ruled by divine providence, then it obviously must also be granted that the "universe is governed by the divine reason."[22] But recall that "law is nothing else but a dictate of practical reason emanating from the ruler who governs a perfect community."[23] Therefore, "the very notion of the government of things in God, the ruler of the universe, has the nature of a law."[24] And since the divine reason's conception of things is not subject to time, but is eternal, God's law is eternal.

We surely can, and in some context should, raise skeptical questions about God and providence. However, for the sake of the present argument, let us assume that there actually exists that reality, whatever it may be, that Jews, Christians, and Moslems call God. Now let us ask how we can know that we ought to do what God commands. What we need to say is this: If God commanded (via revelation, the pope or whatever) that everyone do X, then Jews, Christians, Moslems, and the like would *feel* obligated to do X, *whatever* X might be. A Jew, Christian, or Moslem is never free to question the will of God. What God commands is for him *normative*, i.e., the thing to do. This is in a broad sense a definitional matter; it holds in virtue of what it means to be "a Christian" or "a Jew" or "a Moslem." But to return to what has been thought by one Catholic philosopher to be an insane question, why shouldn't the will of God be questioned? The *Jew, Christian* or *Moslem* cannot question God's will, because each views God as the *perfect good.* Such a religious man would not call a reality 'God' that he did not take to be supremely good and supremely worthy of worship.

It isn't that man judges God—that is indeed blasphemy—but what is true is that no reality, no force or being or world ground, no matter how powerful or eternal, would be called 'God' unless that reality were taken to be good by the agent making that judgment. That is to say, before we can appropriately use the word 'God'—given the meaning it has in developed Jewish, Christian, and Moslem discourse—to characterize that reality— e.g., that force, being, or world ground—we must already have made a judgment about its goodness. This shows that our concept of goodness and our criteria for goodness are prior to and not dependent on our belief in the existence of some 'world ground' or 'transcendent being'. Since this is so, no one can get one's exemplar, one's model for what one ought to be and do, from simply knowing that a totally unlimited being exists who created all other beings and was not created himself. A knowledge that such an esoteric metaphysical reality exists, if indeed it exists or even could exist, would not of itself tell us that we ought to do what is good or tell us what is good. And that such a being issues commands does not invest these commands with moral authority, unless one judges that the being is God, i.e., that the being, the 'world ground', is *worthy* of absolute obedience, that the being is *wholly and perfectly good.* But then one must do just that; one cannot just somehow see what is good through becoming aware that there is a supremely powerful and intelligent creator of the world. (Intelligence and power, even supremely intelligent and powerful people, can still be evil.) But then, *apropos* morality and, if you will, natural moral law, man becomes the measure of all things. One is forced—logically forced—into what Jacques Maritain regards as a rationalistic deformation of the concepts of natural law, rather than into the theocratic position that Aquinas wanted to defend.[25] Man, as far as morality is concerned, ultimately becomes the measure of all things. And it is just this, of course, that Thomistic defenders of the natural moral law wish to avoid.

Yet, perhaps in some way there is natural moral law? That is, there may be, as Aquinas thinks, an unwritten law "whereby each one knows, and is conscious of, what is good and what is evil."[26] It is Aquinas's belief that we are aware of such law through our natural inclinations. That is to say, through these inclinations we are aware of our *proper* end. Indeed, this "natural law is nothing else than the rational creature's participation in the eternal law." But we are aware of what the natural law is, of what is good and evil, through the use of our natural *practical* reason. If we will but honestly heed our *natural* inclinations, we will become aware of what it is that we ought to do.

As John Stuart Mill has classically argued, it is not clear how we can, without in effect appealing to some unexpressed moral standard not derived from nature, determine what is natural and unnatural here.[27] Moreover, it would seem to be the case that sometimes our "natural inclinations" are good and sometimes they are bad and that we require a standard, distinct from our natural inclinations, to ascertain when this is so. And it remains thoroughly unclear how the having of certain *inclinations* could be a form of knowledge. Isn't this just a disguised way of talking about something that is not a matter of knowledge at all but of how we feel or what pro-attitudes we happen to have?

However, even if all these difficulties are somehow overcome, it should still be remembered that natural law, even for Aquinas, will not cover all areas of human conduct. It gives us a *general* determination of how we should act, but it will not give us a particular determination of all or even most of the determinate ordinances we need in a particular society. Here we need human reason and human positive law. For these rules, Aquinas agrees, man is the measure of all things. Indeed no human law, if it is genuine law, can conflict with natural law, but the natural law by itself is not adequate for a rational determination of how we ought to live.

Recall that the eternal law, of which the natural law is a part, "is the supreme exemplar to which we must always conform."[28] "It," Aquinas would have us believe, "is nothing else than the exemplar of the divine wisdom, as directing all actions and movements."[29] We cannot, of course, know the "eternal law as it is in itself . . . for we cannot know the essence of God. But all men, at least to a certain extent, in virtue of their common humanity, have a knowledge of the natural law."[30] But the point is that it has not been shown how or even that this alleged common humanity provides a foundation for moral knowledge or a criterion of good and evil.

There are, however, some further arguments about such an

appeal to natural law that bear examining. There are, Aquinas argues, several precepts of the natural law. They are the first self-evident principles of the practical reason. Now, Aquinas says, a "proposition is said to be self-evident in itself if its predicate is contained in the notion of the subject. . . ."[31] That is to say, such a proposition is analytic. Aquinas readily admits that if people do not know the meaning of the subject term, they will not recognize that such a proposition is self-evident, but all the same, if the predicate is contained in the idea of the subject, it is actually self-evident. These propositions are said by Aquinas to be self-evident *in themselves*. The following are plain cases of self-evident propositions, propositions that anyone with a mastery of language recognizes to be self-evident.

(1) Every whole is greater than its parts.

(2) Things equal to one and the same thing are equal to one another.

By contrast, proposition (3) below is said to be self-evident *in itself*, but not self-evident to everyone.

(3) An angel is not circumscriptively in a place.

Propositions like (3) are only *known* by the wise to be self-evident. But, such propositions, after all, have the same logical status as (1) and (2). They are analytic. As such they are empirically empty, for they rest on linguistic conventions; they exhibit our determination to use words in a certain way. They do not inform us of the existence of some unique reality.

Turning now to Aquinas's self-evident principles of the natural law, we can readily see how empty they are. He remarks, ". . . as being is the first thing that falls under the apprehension absolutely, so *good* is the first thing that falls under the apprehension of the practical reason. . . ."[32] Consequently, "the first principle in the practical reason is one founded on the nature of the good, *viz., that good is that which all things seek after.* Hence, this is the first precept of law, that good is to be done and promoted and evil is to be avoided."[33]

Again, as was the case with our earlier analytic propositions, we have something that is utterly empty. It is self-evidently certain only because it is analytic. We would not all call something good unless we were also prepared to say it is something that is, *ceteris paribus,* to be done. Similarly, if we say that something is evil, we also give to understand that it is something that, *ceteris paribus,* is to be avoided. These remarks make explicit how it is we use the terms 'good' and 'evil' or, as in Aquinas's case, how the Latin equivalents were used. It gives us some insight into the workings of our language, but, as with all tautologies, it is still utterly empty. It does not tell us *what* is good or *what* is evil and a knowledge of this key principle of the natural law does not enable us to work out what is good or what is evil. That is to say, it does not give us any knowledge of good and evil. We only learn what we would know anyway if we understand how to use 'good' and 'evil', namely, that if something is good it is, *ceteris paribus,* to be done and if something is evil, it is, *ceteris paribus,* to be avoided. The price of self-evidence here is utter emptiness.

Yet, Aquinas claims that "all other precepts of the natural law are based upon the first precept of the natural law."[34] But how can this possibly be, for from an analytic proposition, only analytic propositions can be derived. If Aquinas was right, all of the other precepts of the natural law would also be empty.

It is indeed true that Aquinas attempts to give content to the natural law by bringing in *natural inclinations.*[35] Good, he tells us, "has the nature of an end. . . ." All those things toward which "man has a natural inclination are naturally apprehended by reason as good, and consequently as objects of pursuit, and their contraries as evil, and the objects of avoidance. Therefore the order of the precepts of the natural law is according to the order of natural inclinations."[36]

I have already exhibited some of the objections to such a claim, but in addition we need to ask how Aquinas knows, or indeed does he know, that 'All those things to which man has a natural inclination are naturally apprehended by reason as being good' is true? It is surely not self-evident, for 'Some natural inclinations are bad' is not self-contradictory or even logically odd. Vanity, love of power, acquisitiveness, even cruelty seem to be natural inclinations, yet they are surely undesirable human traits.[37] That they are more common in societies that are enculturated into possessive individualism does not prove that they are not natural human traits or, if it does, then it is very unlikely that much of anything is natural. Furthermore—ringing some changes on G. E. Moore—if we say 'good' *means* 'what we have a natural inclination toward', we surely make a mistake, for 'He has a natural inclination toward x, but is x good?' and 'People are naturally inclined toward x, but x is evil' are both perfectly nondeviant utterances, but they would not be if 'good' meant 'what we have a natural inclination toward'.

Aquinas also makes a different argument. He contends that, as with all things, human beings, in acting in accordance with their nature, seek self-preservation. But (*a*) this is not universally true and (*b*) even if they always do, why is it a good thing that they *always* so act? It is not clear that self-preservation *under any circumstance* is always a good thing. Moreover—and as an utterly distinct point—human beings share many inclinations with other animals. How do we know, or do we know, that all these inclinations are good? And how do we know, alternatively, that those inclinations *distinctive* of the human animal are good? In both cases—to put it mildly—we have grounds for skepticism.

Finally, and as a distinct point showing how law and morality cannot be identified, there have been laws made not for the common good but for individual benefit and for the benefit of small groups or dominant classes. Rockefeller, Krupp, Carnegie, and others were and are adept at having this done. It is doubtful whether the Middle Ages was any better in that respect. Aquinas seems implicitly to recognize this when he remarks, "law is chiefly ordained to the common good."[38] But Aquinas vacillates when he goes on to say that any law not for the common good is not really law. Couldn't an Austin quite properly reply, "It's a law all right only it ought not to be. It is a law that ought to be repealed"? Even if we agree, that law is a rule of reason, what evidence do we have that all law is for the common good? Evil and oppressive laws are, to put it bluntly, still laws. It very much appears at least to be the case that the Thomistic conception of the natural law is a myth.

VII

The kind of criticism that I and others have made of natural law conceptions has met with stiff resistance.[39] It has been thought by some that at best we have refuted certain theological or metaphysical articulations of natural law conceptions, but that a viable, if somewhat diminished, natural law theory can and should be stated, defended, and developed quite independently of such obscure metaphysical structures.[40] Not all natural law conceptions, it is argued, are mythical.

Let us see if this is so. More particularly, let us see if a persuasive case can be made for claiming that there are a set of moral principles *properly called laws* that (1) give a minimum moral content to anything that is correctly called 'law' and (2) can serve as an objective standard for moral criticism of institutions and 'positive law'. That is to say, it can provide us with a decision procedure for deciding whether certain putative 'positive laws' are genuine laws or for deciding whether an alleged legal system is genuine. (I have scare quotes around 'positive law' because I suspect that 'positive law' is pleonastic.) The essential issue can be put in another way: Do we have good reasons for believing that there are natural moral laws— objective, unchangeable, normative *laws*—that everywhere and at all times serve as a measure or criterion for the behavior, legal and otherwise, of human beings? Are there such natural laws that determine what can be law in any society and determine, as well, what people can rightly do?

William Frankena's "On Defining and Defending Natural Law" is a sophisticated attempt to show that there are such natural laws.[41] Frankena first notes that when natural law is being defended or attacked, it is a mistake to take it to be the case that, like the fugitive slave laws or immigration laws or tax laws, a law or set of laws is being attacked or defended. That is, in defending natural law, we are not defending a law but a conception of what constitutes law. After all, in ordinary contexts, when one attacks something, one presupposes that it exists, but in discussing natural law, what is precisely at issue is whether there is or can be a law that is natural. Here we are not discussing a law but a thesis *about* law; "not a legal question, but a meta-legal one."[42]

Is the statement 'There is a law that is natural' either a contradiction in terms or in some other way incoherent? Some will say yes, for a law by definition involves an act of legislative will or perhaps a custom. It cannot be something natural. Here both the words 'law' and 'natural' are troublesome. Following Frankena, let us first consider 'law'. Faced with the above criticism, the proponent of natural law might reply in one or another of three ways. First, like some ethical naturalists, he could correctly argue that we do use 'law' with such a meaning in the sciences. There are, that is, natural laws—statements of invariable regularities—in the physical sciences. Natural moral laws, he could argue, are just such scientific laws or generalizations, though in this case they are about human behavior. Not all factual statements are normative but normative statements are a distinct subspecies of factual statement, i.e., statements that at one and the same time both assert that something is the case and appraise or evaluate that state of affairs. If a defender of the natural moral law makes such a claim, he is arguing for ethical naturalism; to refute him, it might be argued, one must refute ethical naturalism. On the other hand, if such a defender of natural law simply limited himself, as he could, to pointing out that in science there are natural laws and that since this use of 'law' is legitimate, it is possible that, in this not very interesting sense there are natural moral laws as well. Second, a defender of natural moral law might grant that natural moral laws are not scientific laws and still hold that there are "general norms of conduct" that are quite natural and are properly called 'laws'. I shall return in a moment to this point. Third, a defender of natural moral law might grant that ethical and political principles are not appropriately called laws, but maintain that the gravamen of the so-called natural law argument "is concerned only to maintain that there are general standards of conduct that are 'natural'."[43]

This is an interesting and new way of looking at the problem, but in spite of my admiration for Frankena's clarity and sense of alternatives, it seems to me that when we get to his "essential natural law man" it includes anyone who rejects ethical relativism, conventionalism, or subjectivism.[44] He, like Alf Ross, assumes that any cognitivist in meta-ethics is committed to a natural law position.[45] On Frankena's position, I should be taken

as a defender of natural law and the pragmatists John Dewey
and Sidney Hook should be taken to be defenders of natural
law. Worse still, the classical arch opponents of natural law,
Bentham, Austin, and Mill, should also be taken as really being
natural law philosophers. But this is conversion by stipulative
redefinition. Indeed, natural law has many mansions but if we
use the expression "natural law philosophers" in such a wide
way that the most paradigmatic opponents of natural law become natural law philosophers, we must have misused the terms
'natural law' and 'natural moral law philosopher'. Frankena is
a clear-headed, able philosopher and not a woolly head like Paul
Tillich, but here he has done for 'natural law' what Tillich does
for 'religion', namely, he has so extended its meaning that it
clearly includes things that it ought not to include.[46]

Yet, the soundness of that point notwithstanding, Frankena
has some important points to make, so let us carefully examine
his analysis. Frankena considers the position of the person who
is taking the second defense of natural law described above.
Let us, for the time being, assume that he has established that
there are certain naturally known, universally true moral principles. Let us take M, N, and O as examples.

M: We ought to love our fellowmen.

N: All men ought to be treated equally.

O: Everyone has the right to life, liberty, and security of
person.

M, N, and O are taken, on this account, as instances of natural
moral laws. Now if the natural moral law philosopher is taking
the second possibility I described above, he must believe that
M, N, and O are not merely universally valid moral principles,
but that they must be *laws* as well, though they need not be
embodied in or enforced by any legal system in order to be
laws. Aquinas and his followers, for example, would say that
M, N, and O are natural laws because they are commanded
by God, though "what is enjoined in them is not right because
it is commanded by God, but is commanded by God because
it is right."[47] Thus M, N, and O are not simply universal moral
principles; they are also laws because they are *ordinances* of

God, and they are *natural* laws because they *order* us to do what also can quite naturally be recognized as the right thing to do.

To this, it may be objected, as Frankena points out himself, that it still does not follow that *as laws*, these moral principles are natural. M, N, and O are naturally known to be true moral principles and, as God's commands, they are known as laws, but they are not just naturally *laws*, as they are just naturally valid moral principles, even if there is no God. Rather, they become *laws* because they are commanded by God.

However, in spite of this, there remains, Frankena argues, a good sense in which M, N, and O can be taken to be natural laws. Natural law, as distinct from divine law, is the law of God known to be God's law naturally and not by means of revelation. Fastening on this, such a proponent of the natural law, "may argue, first, that God being righteous, we can be certain that He will command and enforce what is right; second, that we can know this by our natural faculties, and also that M, N, and O state what is right; third, that we can therefore know by our natural faculties that M, N, and O are laws; and hence, finally, that M, N, and O are natural laws in a perfectly good sense. What they call for is naturally known both to be naturally right and to be the law."[48] Frankena points out that to attack this position, we need to show any one of the following: (1) that nothing can be naturally right, (2) that nothing can be commanded by God on this ground, or (3) naturally known to be commanded by God.

The short answer here is that we do not have good reasons for believing that there is a God who issues commands. At least, given the development of philosophy since the Enlightenment, the burden of proof is very much on the part of the believer to give us some reasons for thinking that belief in God is rationally justified or even that the concept of God is a coherent concept.[49] Moreover, even assuming there is some totally independent being upon whom all other beings depend, we still have no reason to believe we have a natural knowledge of such a deity or of His commands. In short, such conceptions of natural law have such a myth-laden basis that they can hardly be taken at face value.

Frankena, after considering a kind of theological volunteerism, which would only give us another baseless ground for accepting natural law, sets out and defends a secular nonmetaphysical statement of natural law.

> Suppose a philosopher subscribes to MNO and holds (x) that they are expressions of attitude, not true or false statements; (y) that they and the attitudes expressed in them are nevertheless justifiable by reference to naturally known facts about man and the world; and (z) that they provide a basis for evaluating all human codes, institutions, laws, and the like. Is he a natural law theorist or not? He is certainly asserting some of these in the natural law tradition, namely (y) and (z). And is it so clear that (x) is incompatible with the tradition?[51]

Not even an emotivist need reject such a position. But on what grounds could he say M, N, and O are *laws*? They are fundamental moral principles that we subscribe to and they are, if this account is correct, justified on the basis of our knowledge of man and the world. We could *make* them laws by incorporating them into our legal system. But until they are so incorporated, they cannot intelligibly be called 'laws'. But then they are hardly natural *laws*. The difficulty, conceptually, is to get 'natural' and 'laws' coherently together.

In the theological versions of natural law, these laws were ordinances and commands of God; assuming that we are justified in believing in God, this made it at least somewhat plausible to say they are laws. But in this secular version, why should we say they are *laws* rather than simply say they are fundamental moral principles or indeed just fundamental moral commitments? What is there about them that justifies the secular nonmetaphysical defender of natural moral law in calling them laws? How could we show an opponent to be mistaken who claimed that they were simply fundamental moral principles that no *morally* justified legal system could flout? How could he show that M, N, and O were, after all, really laws? They are, evidently enough, either moral principles or moral commitments and are unlike human laws or laws of nature. What grounds have we for calling them laws? To call them laws seems simply to confuse matters.

In an effort to find possible ways of getting around this, let us consider the following claim: there are valid principles about duties and rights that are natural. Frankena says that the key words here are 'valid' and 'natural'. There are two things we can plausibly mean here by 'valid'. (1) We can mean that these ethical principles are true. However, some noncognitivists or error theorists would deny that anything like this can be correctly said. (2) Alternatively, we can say that to assert that these are valid moral principles is to assert the existence of ethical principles that are justified or rationally acceptable even though they do not ascribe properties to things or assert relations between them. Defenders of natural law have historically argued that these principles are valid in the sense of being *true*, but if they were to adopt this second position, would they really be altering their position in any essential way? Frankena does *not* think they would. This is surely a jarring note on the meta-conceptions of at least most of those who regard themselves as part of the natural law tradition. But would it really make much difference to anything of moral substance?

Frankena next considers in what sense such principles could be said to be natural. He gives three distinct senses. (1) There are valid moral principles that ascribe rights and duties to persons simply by virtue of their status as human beings. A moralist who holds such a view might proceed on the following basis: "I am a human being and I do not regard as morally relevant mere tribal differences between myself and other human beings." A person's freedom ought to be respected simply because he is a person. A person's life needs to be respected simply because he is a human being, and in virtue of this he deserves a fair trial and a certain kind of equitable treatment. In that way moral judgments are natural. (This seems to me, by the way, a rather odd use of 'natural'.) (2) The justifiability or truth of moral principles of even this fundamental sort can be established by our natural faculties.[52] That is to say, human intelligence and experience can show us which ones are true. In this way they are natural. But it needs also to be noted that exactly how this is done, if indeed anything like this can be done, can be and has been, variously interpreted. It need not commit one to rationalism in ethics.[53]

It is natural to object that this is a rather empty or vacuous sense of 'natural'. When we say that we establish the correctness of M, N, and O by the use of our natural faculties—our intelligence and experience—what work does 'natural' do? Is not 'natural faculties' pleonastic here? Do we have conventional faculties or supernatural faculties or prenatural faculties? There is no nonvacuous contrast here so it seems at least plausible to say that Frankena is not saying anything.

I think Frankena could respond as follows: "The contrast I had in mind is this: apart from revelation or simply subscribing to a convention or—as the existentialists would have it—making an arbitrary choice, we can, by using our intelligence and through our experience in life, come to know that certain moral principles, e.g., M, N, and O, are justified." Frankena might echo a remark made by the civil rights leader Robert Moses to Robert Penn Warren. There are "unsophisticated people who come off the land," who "simply voice, time and time again, the simple truths you cannot ignore because they speak from their own lives." I do not mean to suggest a kind of Rousseauian primitivism, but it does seem to me that Frankena is claiming that there are some reasonably simple and fundamental moral principles that we could all discover by using our heads *and* by taking to heart our own experience in living. He contrasts this with the claim that there are no such fundamental moral principles. That is, he contrasts this with the claim that M, N, and O are simply ancient mores or conventions, simply principles to which we arbitrarily subscribe or fail to subscribe or are simply the revealed will of some deity. Thus, there is, after all, a nonvacuous contrast here. This is an important and central point, though it is also important to see that it does not show that the moral beliefs we come to subscribe to in this way naturally are also natural *laws*.

Frankena's third sense in which these moral principles would plausibly be said to be natural is this: (3) Fundamental moral principles, e.g., M, N, and O, are true because they logically follow from certain statements of nonmoral fact about human nature or about the world. These nonmoral facts are themselves known through our natural faculties. This, of course, involves deriving an 'ought' from an 'is'.[54] Frankena stresses that traditionally this has been taken as one of the defining features of a natural law theory. It is, of course, very problematical whether such a derivation can be made. But in attempting to find a version of it that is free from these difficulties, Frankena suggests that even this traditional element may not be necessary. Someone who denied that we could derive an 'ought' from an 'is' could still assert that certain fundamental moral claims— M, N, and O, for example—are justified and naturally known. Perhaps this is enough to hold a minimal natural law theory.

Finally, there are three further theses that are essential to any theory of natural moral law. They follow from (1), (2), and (3) above.

(4) Our rights and duties do not depend wholly on the offices we hold, the agreements we have made, the commands addressed to us, or the positive laws that exist.[55]

(5) There are valid moral principles in the light of which we may criticize and appraise all human institutions, laws, codes, actions, and so forth.

(6) "There are ethical principles that hold even in a state of nature."[56]

It is Frankena's claim that if one accepts any of these six theses, on any of their interpretations, one "believes in natural law."[57] These theses are all meta-ethical theses—though they are compatible with a variety of meta-ethical theories—but there are also distinctive normative ethical principles that belong to the natural law tradition. M, N, and O are such principles. They are principles that could easily be multiplied.[58]

Finally, Frankena, in pulling these diverse threads together, suggests what he takes to be a minimal set of criteria for determining what constitutes acceptance of a natural law position. Many people who believe in natural law will believe in other more exotic metaphysical and theological considerations, but to be a natural law person, one must, at least, accept as correct, the theses that Frankena states. And, he claims, they are sufficient to delineate adequately the core of that position. If these theses are accepted, one can reasonably be called a believer in natural moral law. Frankena's criteria are the following:

(I) He subscribes to ethical principles such as M, N, and O.

(II) He holds (a) that we are justified in accepting them, directly or indirectly, by truths known by our natural faculties (though not necessarily by logical deduction); (b) that they justifiably ascribe rights and obligations to all men as such, independently of their offices, agreements, laws, or whatever; and (c) that they may therefore serve as a standard by which to measure all human institutions, rules, and actions.[59]

These Frankena takes as the "important doctrines in the natural law tradition to be for or against."[60] These and only these are essential to the natural law tradition.

As I remarked initially, it seems to me that Frankena has so diluted the natural law tradition as to make it identifiable with any nonconventionalist, nonsubjectivist theory or view of morality. He has given us a low redefinition of 'natural law theory'.[61] What he does here is comparable to defining an 'M.D.' as a person capable of giving first aid. Surely all M.D.s are, in theory at least, capable of doing this, but they are—in order to be M.D.s—capable, in theory at least, of doing much more as well. That is why it is a low redefinition of 'M.D.'. Similarly, natural lawists (if that is the right word) accept the theses Frankena ascribes to them, but to be natural lawists, they must accept some further rather more distinctive and rather more controversial theses as well.

Some may say that this is mere dogmatic counter-assertion on my part. I think there is one reasonably simple way of showing that it is not. Someone might say that Frankena and I are battling over what, if any, characteristics are common to and distinctive of everything properly connoted by the phrase 'natural law'. But 'natural law' has a denotation as well and 'natural law philosophers' also has a denotation as well as a connotation. If Frankena's conception fails to make anyone who is properly referred to as a natural law theorist, a natural law theorist, then there is something wrong with his characterization of natural law. If, for example, Aquinas, Cicero, or Grotius did not fit his characterization, then his characterization is plainly wrong. Similarly, if his characterization includes some figures who are paradigms of philosophers who are not natural lawists, then there is something wrong with his characterization of 'natural law'. But it seems to me that Frankena's account does just that. Namely, on such a conception, Mill, Austin, and Bentham—arch opponents of natural law—become natural law philosophers. But, if this is so, then Frankena's conception of 'natural law' cannot be right, because it includes things under natural law that plainly do not belong there. My low redefinition of 'M.D.' automatically makes a sailor who is a pharmacist's mate an M.D., and thus is *ipso facto* wrong. Frankena's definition of 'natural law' makes Mill a natural law philosopher and thus it follows that Frankena's characterization must be wrong.

It seems to me that one would have to add three more theses to Frankena's list. Let us call them:

(7) Objective ethical principles like M, N, and O are also in some significant sense unchangeable *laws*, valid for all persons and all nations and at all times.

(8) That these laws, which are also ethical principles, are essentially and necessarily part of anything that could, with *conceptual* propriety, be called a legal system.

(9) That these principles can be known to be true or at least justified by coming to know the *natural inclinations* of human beings.

Perhaps we can dispense with (9) in a minimal natural law theory. But (7) and (8) are essential if we are not to get a low redefinition of 'natural law'. But they are both very controversial claims even for ethical objectivists. That is to say, many people who would accept Frankena's theses as justifiable could not accept these. Yet, as far as I can see, (7) and (8), at least, are essential for any natural law theory no matter how demythologized.

I suspect Frankena believes that if we subscribe to (1) and (2), this is really tantamount to accepting (7), unless we want to quibble over the word 'law'. (Recall Frankena says that all people who believe that there are rules or principles about our rights and duties, which are natural, will accept a natural law position, unless they are people who quibble over the use of the term 'law'.)[62] I no more want to quibble over the word 'law' than Frankena. I shall try to show that it is not quibbling over 'law' to refuse the term 'law' for normative ethical principles like M, N, and O.

Remember, to accept (1) and (2) is (a) to accept ethical principles such as 'Everyone has the right to life, liberty, and security of person' and 'All men ought to love their fellowmen' and to believe that (b) such principles are, though sometimes in different ways, justified by accepting truths known by our natural faculties and that these principles so known serve as standards by which all institutions, rules, and actions are judged.

I think there are various questions we could raise about both (1) and (2) but, setting them aside, I want to argue here that the acceptance of (1) and (2) does not commit us to an acceptance of (7). I might very firmly believe that we all ought to love our fellowmen and not think that it is a law or indeed even firmly deny that it either is or should be a law. Alternatively, I might think that it should be a law and deny that it in fact is. I might say, perhaps using H. L. A. Hart's test for what a law is, "Nowhere is it a requirement of the legal system that we all ought to love each other but it should be" or, rather more realistically, I might say "We ought to love each other but that plainly is not the sort of thing that could ever be made part of the legal system" or, to take still another alternative, I could say "I concede that we ought all to love one another, but, human nature being what it is, that could never be made a law." All of these claims might be false or not clearly true or false. However, since they clearly are non-deviant English utterances that seemingly could be used to make intelligible claims, it cannot be the case that we can, without a good deal more argument, legitimately claim that (1) and (2) show that principles such as (1) allows must be taken to be laws. We could accept (1), which involves accepting the sort of principles included in (1), and the rationale for such an acceptance of (1), as given in (2), and still coherently deny that those principles given in (1) are laws.

The burden of proof is on the natural law theorist to show, our plain uses of language notwithstanding, that these so-called natural moral laws are really laws, appearances to the contrary notwithstanding. But Frankena gives us no such argument and no argument has been forthcoming from the natural law tradition.

What I think they are doing, though for the most part unwittingly, is trying to get the *authority* of law out of firm moral convictions. But it is one thing for something to be a moral conviction, even a firm moral conviction; it is something else again for it to be a law. It isn't that one is higher or lower than the other, it is just that they are different. As G. E. Moore, echoing Butler, might have said "Everything is what it is and not another thing. Laws are one thing and moral convictions are another and neither can be reduced to the other." But what is importantly the case is that moral convictions cannot rest on *authority* in the way that laws can.[63] If one could turn these fundamental considered convictions—these considered judgments—into laws, then they could be said to rest on authority or be authoritatively prescribed. But that requires an arbitrary stipulation. It doesn't follow from coming to acknowledge that these fundamental moral principles give expression to very deeply embedded moral convictions that these principles can be authoritatively prescribed. But theories of natural law have not shown how one can make such a derivation here or carry out such a reduction. The natural moral law stands as a consoling fable that tries to give *a type* of objectivity to morality that it does not and cannot possess. But that morality does not have that kind of objectivity does not mean that it does not have any objectivity at all. Moral judgments can have the kind of objectivity rendered by considered judgments in wide reflective equilibrium and that is perhaps the only kind of objectivity they need.[64] We must be on guard against the irrational heart of rationalism and not set out on the quest for certainty. Philosophers and theologians find it very difficult to absorb that lesson.

NOTES

1. Robert Bellah, "Civil Religion in America," *Daedalus* (1967), reprinted in Robert Bellah, *Beyond Belief: Essays on Religion in a Post-Traditional World* (New York: Harper and Row, 1970), pp. 168-86. See also Robert Bellah

and Phillip Hammond, *Varieties of Civil Religion* (San Francisco, Calif.: Harper and Row, 1980); David W. Noble, "Robert Bellah, Civil Religion, and the American Jeremiad," *Soundings* 65, no. 1 (spring 1982): 88-192; and the "Review Symposium on the Sociology of Religion of Robert Bellah," *Journal for the Scientific Study of Religion* 14, no. 4 (1975): 385-414.

2. Kai Nielsen, *Ethics Without God,* 1st ed. (Buffalo, N.Y.: Prometheus Books, 1973).

3. Kai Nielsen, "An Examination of the Thomistic Theory of Natural Moral Law," *Natural Law Forum* 4, no. 1 (1959): 44-71 and my "The Myth of Natural Law" in Sidney Hook (ed.), *Law and Philosophy* (New York: New York University Press, 1964), pp. 122-43.

4. Paul Johnson, "The Necessity for Christianity," address to the Christianity Challenges the University: An International Conference of Theists and Atheists, Dallas, Tex. (7 February 1985). See also his *Modern Times.*

5. John Rawls, *A Theory of Justice* (Cambridge, Mass.: Harvard University Press), pp. 20, 48-51, 120 and 432; and his "Independence of Moral Theory," *Proceedings and Addresses of the American Philosophical Association* 48 (1974-5): 5-22; Jane English, "Ethics and Science," *Proceedings of the XVI International Congress of Philosophy* (1980); Norman Daniels, "Reflective Equilibrium and Archimedean Points," *Canadian Journal of Philosophy* 10, no. 1 (March 1980): 83-104; Norman Daniels, "Wide Reflective Equilibrium and Theory Acceptance in Ethics," *The Journal of Philosophy* 7, no. 5 (May 1979): 256-82; and Kai Nielsen, "Considered Judgements Again," *Human Studies* 5 (1982): 109-18.

6. Kai Nielsen, "On Deriving an Ought from an Is," *Review of Metaphysics* 32, no. 3 (March 1979): 488-515.

7. Bertrand Russell, *Human Society in Ethics and Politics* (New York: Simon and Schuster, 1955), pp. 4-5.

8. Joseph Mercier, *A Manual of Modern Scholastic Philosophy,* Vol II, Part 1, T. L. Parker and S. A. Parker (trans.) (London: Kegan Paul, Trench, Trubner & Co., 1917), chapter 3.

9. Emile Brunner, *The Divine Imperative,* Olive Wyon (trans.) (London: The Westminister Press, 1947), chapters 9 and 11.

10. Mercier, op. cit.

11. F. C. Copleston, *Aquinas* (Baltimore, Md.: Penguin Books, 1955), chapter 5; Clifford G. Kossel, S.J., "The Moral View of Thomas Aquinas," V. Ferm (ed.), *Encyclopedia of Morals* (New York: The Philosophical Library, 1956), pp. 11-23; Jacques Maritain, *Man and the State* (Chicago, Ill.: The University of Chicago Press, 1951); his *The Range of Reason* (New York: Harper and Row, 1951); his "The Natural Law and the Moral Law" in R. N. Anshem (ed.), *Moral Principles of Action* (New York: Harper and Row, 1952), pp. 62-76; and Victor White, "Word of God and Natural Law" in Joseph Katz et al. (eds.), *Writers on Ethics* (Princeton, N.J.: Princeton University Press, 1962).

12. Mercier, op. cit.

13. Ibid.

14. Ibid.

15. St. Thomas Aquinas, *Summa Theologiae I-II* Qg. 90-108. See also his *Summa Contra Gentiles,* Book III.

16. Ibid.

17. Ibid.

18. Ibid.
19. Ibid.
20. Ibid.
21. Ibid.
22. Ibid.
23. Ibid.
24. Ibid.
25. Jacques Maritain, "The Natural Law and the Moral Law."
26. Aquinas, op. cit.
27. J. S. Mill, *Essays on Ethics, Religion and Society,* Collected works, Vol. X (Toronto, Ont: University of Toronto Press, 1969), pp. 373-402.
28. Aquinas, op. cit.
29. Ibid.
30. Ibid.
31. Ibid.
32. Ibid.
33. Ibid.
34. Ibid.
35. Ibid.
36. Ibid.
37. Bertrand Russell, op. cit., pp. 137-58.
38. Aquinas, op. cit.
39. See the essays by Stuart Brown, William K. Frankena, and Kenneth Stern, all in Sidney Hook (ed.), *Law and Philosophy* (New York: New York University Press, 1964).
40. W. K. Frankena, "On Defining and Defending Natural Law," in Sidney Hook (ed.), *Law and Philosophy,* pp. 200-209. See also Alexandre Passerin D'Entreve, "A Core of Good Sense," *Revue Internationale de Philosophie* 17, no. 65 (1965): 271-85.
41. Frankena, op. cit.
42. Ibid.
43. Ibid., p. 201. Frankena spells out carefully the position he must take on pp. 201-202.
44. Ibid.
45. Alf Ross, "Validity and the Conflict Between Legal Positivism and Natural Law," *Revista Juridica de Buenos Aires* 4 (1961): 64-66; and his *On Law and Justice,* (Berkeley, Calif.: University of California Press, 1959), chapters 10 and 11.
46. Kai Nielsen, "Is God so Powerful that He Doesn't Have to Exist?" in Sidney Hook (ed.), *Religious Experience and Truth* (New York: New York University Press, 1961).
47. Frankena, op. cit., p. 202.
48. Ibid.
49. I have raised a challenge about the coherence of God-talk in my *An Introduction to the Philosophy of Religion* (London: Macmillan Press, Ltd., 1982) and in my *Scepticism* (London: Macmillan Press, 1973). And I have criticized attempts to prove, demonstratively or empirically that there is a God in my *Reason and Practice* (New York: Harper and Row, 1971), Part III. J. L. Mackie in a sustained and probing way argues that the various attempts to give us good grounds for believing in the existence of God fail. I think these activities by contemporary philosophers are essentially mopping-

up operations in the wake of the philosophical and scientific developments since the Enlightenment. J. L. Mackie, *The Miracle of Theism* (Oxford, England: Clarendon Press, 1982).

50. Kai Nielsen, "The Myth of Natural Law."

51. Frankena, op. cit., p. 204.

52. To catch the hidden underlying ideology of this, note that 'natural faculties' seems to be pleonastic.

53. For some arguments concerning how broken-backed ethical rationalism is, see Kai Nielsen, "Against Ethical Rationalism," Edward Regis Jr., *Gewirth's Ethical Rationalism* (Chicago, Ill.: The University of Chicago Press, 1984), pp. 59-83.

54. I have argued that we cannot in any significant sense derive an ought from an is in my "Why There is a Problem about Ethics," *The Danish Yearbook* (1978) and in my "On Deriving an Ought from an Is," *Review of Metaphysics* 32, no. 3 (March 1979): 488-515.

55. Frankena, op. cit., p. 206.

56. Ibid., p. 206.

57. Ibid., p. 207.

58. H. A. Rommen gives some other examples in his "In Defense of Natural Law," in Sidney Hook (ed.), *Law and Philosophy* (New York: New York University Press, 1964), pp. 118-19.

59. Frankena, op. cit., p. 209.

60. Ibid.

61. For an explication of the notion of 'low redefinition' see Paul Edwards, *The Logic of Moral Discourse* (Glencoe, Ill.: The Free Press, 1955).

62. Frankena, op. cit., p. 204.

63. Kurt Baier has clearly shown some of the important conceptual differences here in his, *The Moral Point of View* (Ithaca, N.Y.: Cornell University Press, 1958), pp. 127-39.

64. Thomas Nagel, in a probing essay, shows how we must be wary of importing into the domain of the moral, conceptions of objectivity that have no place there. Thomas Nagel, "The Limits of Objectivity," in Sterling M. McMurrin (ed.), *The Tanner Lectures on Human Values* (1980) (Salt Lake City, Utah: University of Utah Press, 1980), pp. 77-139.

2

Morality and the Will of God

I

It is the claim of many influential Jewish and Christian theologians (Brunner, Buber, Barth, Niebuhr, and Bultmann—to take outstanding examples) that the only genuine basis for morality is in religion. And any old religion is not good enough. The only truly adequate foundation for moral belief is a religion that acknowledges the absolute sovereignty of the Lord found in the prophetic religions.

These theologians will readily grant what is plainly true, namely, that as a matter of fact many nonreligious people behave morally, but they contend that without a belief in God and his law there is no ground or reason for being moral. The sense of moral relativism, skepticism, and nihilism rampant in our age is due in large measure to the general weakening of religious belief in an age of science. Without God there can be no objective foundation for our moral beliefs. As Brunner puts it, "The believer alone clearly perceives that the Good, as it is recognized in faith, is the sole Good, and all that is otherwise called good cannot lay claim to this title, at least in the ultimate sense of the word . . . The Good consists in always doing what God wills at any particular moment."[1] Moreover, this moral Good can only be attained by our 'unconditional obedience' to God, the ground of our being. Without God life would have no

51

point and morality would have no basis. Without religious belief, without the Living God, there could be no adequate answer to the persistently gnawing questions: What ought we to do? How ought I to live?

Is this frequently repeated claim justified? Are our moral beliefs and conceptions based on or grounded in a belief in the God of Judaism, Christianity, and Islam? In trying to come to grips with this question, we need to ask ourselves three fundamental questions.

(1) Is being willed by God the, or even a, *fundamental* criterion for that which is so willed being morally good or for its being something that ought to be done?

(standard of judgment)

(2) Is being willed by God the *only* criterion for that which is so willed being morally good or for its being something that ought to be done?

(3) Is being willed by God the only *adequate* criterion for that which is so willed being morally good or being something that ought to be done?

I shall argue that the fact that God wills something—if indeed that is a fact—cannot be a fundamental criterion for its being morally good or obligatory and thus it cannot be the only criterion or the only adequate criterion for moral goodness or obligation.

By way of preliminaries we should first get clear what is meant by a fundamental criterion. When we speak of the criterion for the goodness of an action or attitude we speak of some measure or test by virtue of which we may decide which actions or attitudes are good or desirable, or, at least, are the least undesirable of the alternate actions or attitudes open to us. A moral criterion is the measure we use for determining the value or worth of an action, principle, rule, or attitude. We have such a measure or test when we have some generally relevant considerations by which we may decide whether something is whatever it is said to be. A fundamental moral criterion is (*a*) a test or measure used to judge the legitimacy of moral rules and/or acts or attitudes, and (*b*) a measure that one would give up last if one were reasoning morally. (In reality, there probably is no single fundamental criterion, although there are fundamental criteria.)

There is a further preliminary matter we need to consider. In asking about the basis or authority for our moral beliefs we are not asking about how we came to have them. If you ask someone where he got his moral beliefs, he, to be realistic, should answer that he got them from his parents, parent surrogates, teachers.[2] They are beliefs which he has been conditioned to accept. But the validity or soundness of a belief is independent of its origin. When one person naively asks another where he got his moral beliefs, most likely he is not asking how he came by them, but rather, (a) on what authority he holds these beliefs, or (b) what good reasons or justification he has for these moral beliefs. He should answer that he does not and cannot hold these beliefs on any authority. It is indeed true that many of us turn to people for moral advice and guidance in moral matters, but if we do what we do simply because it has been authorized, we cannot be reasoning and acting as moral agents; for to respond as a moral agent, one's moral principle must be something that is subscribed to by one's own deliberate commitment, and it must be something for which one is prepared to give reasons.

Keeping these preliminary clarifications in mind, we can return to my claim that the fact (if indeed it is a fact) that God has commanded, willed or ordained something cannot, in the very nature of the case, be a fundamental criterion for claiming that whatever is commanded, willed, or ordained *ought* to be done.

II

Some perceptive remarks made by A. C. Ewing will carry us part of the way.[3] Theologians like Barth and Brunner claim that ethical principles gain their justification because they are God's decrees. But as Ewing points out, if 'being obligatory' means just 'willed by God', it becomes unintelligible to ask why God wills one thing rather than another. In fact, there can be no reason for his willing one thing rather than another, for his willing it *eo ipso* makes whatever it is he wills good, right, or obligatory. 'God wills it because it ought to be done' becomes 'God wills it because God wills it'; but the first sentence, even as used by the most ardent believer, is not a tautology. "If it were said in reply that God's commands determine what we ought to do but that these commands were only issued because it was good that they should be or because obedience to them did good, this would still make judgments about the good, at least, independent of the will of God, and we should not have given a definition of all fundamental ethical concepts in terms of God or made ethics dependent on God."[4] Furthermore, it becomes senseless to say what the believer very much wants to say, namely, "I ought always to do what God wills" if 'what I ought to do' and 'what God wills' have the same meaning. And to say I ought to do what God wills because I love God makes the independent assumption that I ought to love God and that I ought to do what God wills if I love him.

Suppose we say instead that we ought to do what God wills because God will punish us if we do not obey him. This may indeed be a cogent self-interested or prudential reason for doing what God commands, but it is hardly a morally good reason for doing so since such considerations of self-interest cannot be adequate bases for morality. A powerful being—an omnipotent and omniscient being—speaking out of the whirlwind cannot by his mere commands create an obligation. Ewing goes on to assert: "Without a prior conception of God as good or his commands as right, God would have no more claim on our obedience than Hitler or Stalin except that He would have more power than even they had to make things uncomfortable for those who disobey Him."[5] Unless we assume that God is morally perfect, unless we assume the perfect goodness of God, there can be no necessary "relation between being commanded or willed by God and being obligatory or good."[6]

To this it is perfectly correct to reply that as believers we must believe that God is wholly and completely good, the most perfect of all conceivable beings.[7] It is not open for a Jew or a Christian to question the goodness of God. He must start with that assumption. Any man who seriously questions God's goodness or asks why he should obey God's commands shows by this very response that he is not a Jew or a Christian. Believers must claim that God is wholly and utterly good and that what He wills or commands is of necessity good, though this does not entail that the believer is claiming that the necessity here is a logical necessity. For a believer, God is all good; he is the perfect good. This being so, it would seem that the believer is justified in saying that he and we—if his claim concerning God is correct—ought to do what God wills and that our morality is after all grounded in a belief in God. But this claim of his is clearly dependent on his assumption that God is good. Yet I shall argue that even if God is good, indeed even if God is the perfect good, it does not follow that morality can be based on religion and that we can know what we ought to do simply by knowing what God wishes us to do.

III

To come to understand the grounds for this last rather elliptical claim, we must consider the logical status of 'God is good'. Is it a nonanalytic and in some way substantive claim, or is it analytic? (Can we say that it is neither?) No matter what we say, we get into difficulties.

Let us first try to claim that it is nonanalytic, that it is in some way a substantive statement. So understood, God cannot then be by definition good. If the statement is synthetic and substantive, its denial cannot be self-contradictory; that is, it cannot be self-contradictory to assert that X is God but X is not good. It would always in fact be wrong to assert this, for God is the perfect good. But the denial of this claim is not self-contradictory, it is just false or in some way mistaken. The 'is' in 'God is the perfect good' is not the 'is' of identity, perfect goodness is being predicated of God in some logically contingent way. It is the religious experience of the believer and the events recorded in the Bible that lead the believer to the steadfast conviction that God has a purpose or vocation for him which he can fulfill only by completely submitting to God's will. God shall lead him and guide him in every thought, word, and deed. Otherwise he will be like a man shipwrecked, lost in a vast and indifferent universe. Through careful attention to the Bible, he comes to understand that God is a wholly good being who has dealt faithfully with his chosen people. God is not by definition perfectly good or even good, but in reality, though not of logical necessity, he never falls short of perfection.

Assuming that 'God is good' is not a truth of language, how, then, do we know that God is good? Do we know or have good grounds for believing that the remarks made at the end of the above paragraph are so? The believer can indeed make such a claim, but how do we or how does he know that this is so? What grounds have we for believing that God is good? Naïve people, recalling how God spoke to Job out of the whirlwind, may say that God is good because he is omnipotent and omniscient. But this clearly will not do, for, as Hepburn points out, there is nothing logically improper about saying "X is omnipotent and omniscient and morally wicked."[8] Surely in the world as we know it there is no logical connection between being powerful and knowledgeable and being good. As far as I can see, all that God proved to Job, when he spoke to him out of the whirlwind was that God was an immeasurably powerful being; but he did not prove his moral superiority to Job, and he did nothing at all even to exhibit his moral goodness. (One might even argue that he exhibited moral wickedness.) We need not assume that omnipotence and omniscience bring with them goodness or even wisdom.

What other reason could we have for claiming that God is good? We might say that he is good because he tells us to do good in thought, word, and deed and to love one another. In short, in his life and in his precepts God exhibits for us his goodness and love. Now one might argue that children's hospitals and concentration camps clearly show that such a claim is false. But let us assume that in some way God does exhibit his goodness to man. Let us assume that if we examine God's works we cannot but affirm that God is good.[9] We come to understand that he is not cruel, callous, or indifferent. But in order to make such judgments or to gain such an understanding, we must use our own logically independent moral criteria. In taking God's goodness as not being true by definition or as being some kind of conceptual truth, we have, in asserting 'God is good', of necessity made a moral judgment, a moral appraisal, using a criterion that cannot be based on a knowledge that God exists or that he issues commands. We call God good because we have experienced the goodness of his acts, but in order to do this, in order to know that he is good or to have any grounds for believing that he is good, we must have an independent moral criterion that we use in making this predication of God. So if 'God is good' is taken to be synthetic and substantive, then morality cannot simply be based on a belief in God. We must of logical necessity have some criterion of goodness that is not derived from any statement asserting that there is a deity.

IV

Let us alternatively, and more plausibly, take 'God is good' to be a truth of language. Now some truths of language (some analytic statements) are statements of identity, such as 'puppies are young dogs' or 'a father is a male parent'. Such statements are definitions and the 'is' indicates identity. But 'God is good' is clearly not such a statement of identity, for that 'God' does not have the same meaning as 'good' can easily be seen from the following case: Jane says to Betsy, after Betsy helps an old lady across the street, "That was good of you." 'That was good of you' most certainly does not mean 'that was God of you'. And when we say "conscientiousness is good" we do not mean to say "conscientiousness is God." To say, as a believer does, that God is good is not to say that God is God. This clearly indicates that the word 'God' does not have the same meaning as the word 'good'. When we are talking about God we are not talking simply about morality.

'God is the perfect good' is somewhat closer to 'a father is a male parent', but even here 'God' and 'the perfect good' are not identical in meaning. 'God is the perfect good' in some important respects is like 'a triangle is a trilateral'. Though something is a triangle if and only if it is a trilateral, it does not follow that 'triangle' and 'trilateral' have the same meaning. Similarly, something is God if and only if that something is the perfect good, but it does not follow that 'God' and 'the perfect good' have the same meaning. When we speak of God we wish to say other things about him as well, though indeed what is true of God will also be true of the perfect good. Yet what is true of the evening star will also be true of the morning star, since they both refer to the same object, Venus; but, as Frege has shown, it does not follow that the two terms have the same meaning if they have the same referent.

Even if it could be made out that 'God is the perfect good' is in some way a statement of identity, (a) it would not make 'God is good' a statement of identity, and (b) we could know that X is the perfect good only if we already knew how to decide that X is good.[10] So even on the assumption that 'God is the perfect good' is a statement of identity, we need an independent way of deciding whether something is good; we must have an independent criterion for goodness.

Surely the alternative presently under consideration is more plausible than the alternative considered in section III. 'God is good' most certainly appears to be analytic in the way 'puppies are young', 'a bachelor is unmarried', or 'unjustified killing is wrong' are analytic. These statements are not statements of identity; they are not definitions, though they all follow from definitions and to deny any of them is self-contradictory.

In short, it seems to me correct to maintain that 'God is good', 'puppies are young', and 'triangles are three-sided' are all truths of language; the predicates partially define their subjects. That is to say—to adopt for a moment a Platonic-sounding idiom—goodness is partially definitive of Godhood, as youngness is partially definitive of puppyhood and as three-sidedness is partially definitive of triangularity.

To accept this is not at all to claim that we can have no understanding of good without an understanding of God; and the truth of the above claim that God is good will not show that God is the, or even a, fundamental criterion for goodness. Let us establish first that and then how the fact of such truths of language does not show that we could have no understanding of good without having an understanding of God. We could not understand the full religious sense of what is meant by 'God' without knowing that whatever is denoted by this term is said to be good; but, as 'young' or 'three-sided' are understood without reference to puppies or triangles, though the converse cannot be the case, so 'good' is also understood quite independently of any reference to God. We can intelligibly say, "I have a three-sided figure here that is most certainly not a triangle" and "Colts are young but they are not puppies." Similarly, we can well say "Conscientiousness, under most circumstances at least, is good even in a world without God." Such an utterance is clearly intelligible, to believer and nonbeliever alike. It is a well-formed English sentence with a use in the language. Here we can use the word 'good' without either asserting or assuming the reality of God. Such linguistic evidence clearly shows that 'good' is a concept that can be understood quite independently of any reference to the deity, that morality without religion, without theism, is quite possible. In fact, just the reverse is the case. Christianity, Judaism, and theistic religions of that sort could not exist if people did not have a moral understanding that was, logically speaking, quite independent of such religions. We could have no understanding of the truth of 'God is good' or of the concept God unless we had an independent understanding of goodness.

That this is so can be seen from the following considerations. If we had no understanding of the word 'young', and if we did not know the criteria for deciding whether a dog was young, we could not know how correctly to apply the word 'puppy'. Without such a prior understanding of what it is to be young, we could not understand the sentence "Puppies are young." Similarly, if we had no understanding of the use of the word 'good', and if we did not know the criteria for deciding whether a being (or if you will, a power or a force) was good, we could not know how correctly to apply the word 'God'. Without such a prior understanding of goodness, we could not understand the sentence "God is good." This clearly shows that our understanding of morality and knowledge of goodness are independent of any knowledge that we may or may not have of the divine. Indeed, without a prior and logically independent understanding of good and without some nonreligious criterion for judging something to be good, the religious person could have no knowledge of God, for he could not know whether that powerful being who spoke out of the whirlwind and laid the foundations of the earth was in fact worthy of worship and perfectly good.

From my argument we should conclude that we cannot decide whether something is good or whether it ought to be done simply from finding out (assuming that we can find out) that God commanded it, willed it, enjoined it. Furthermore, whether 'God is good' is synthetic (substantive) or analytic (a truth of language), the concept of good must be understood as something distinct from the concept of God; that is to say, a man could know how to use 'good' properly and still not know how to use 'God'. Conversely, a man could not know how to use 'God' correctly unless he already understood how to use 'good'. An understanding of goodness is logically prior to, and is independent of, any understanding or acknowledgment of God.

V

In attempting to counter my argument for the necessary independence of morality—including a central facet of religious morality—from any beliefs about the existence or powers of the deity, the religious moralist might begin by conceding that (a) there are secular moralities that are logically independent of religion, and (b) that we must understand the meanings of moral terms independently of understanding what it means to speak of God. He might even go so far as to grant that only a man who understood what good and bad were could come to believe in God. 'Good', he might grant, does not mean 'willed by God' or anything like that; and 'there is no God, but human happiness is nonetheless good' is indeed perfectly intelligible as a moral utterance. But granting that, it is still the case that Jew and Christian do and must—on pain of ceasing to be Jew and Christian—take God's will as their final court of appeal in the making of moral appraisals or judgments. Any rule, act, or attitude that conflicts with what the believer sincerely believes to be the will of God must be rejected by him. It is indeed true that in making moral judgments the Jew or Christian does not always use God's will as a criterion for what is good or what ought to be done. When he says "Fluoridation is a good thing" or "The resumption of nuclear testing is a crime," he need not be using God's will as a criterion for his moral judgment. But where any moral judgment or any other moral criterion conflicts with God's ordinances, or with what the person making the judgment honestly takes to be God's ordinances, he must accept those ordinances, or he is no longer a Jew or a Christian. In this way, God's will is his fundamental moral criterion.

That the orthodox Jew or Christian would reason in this way is perfectly true, but though he says that God's will is his fundamental criterion, it is still plain that he has a yet more fundamental criterion that he must use in order to employ God's will as a moral criterion. Such a religious moralist must believe and thus be prepared to make the moral claim that there exists a being whom he deems to be perfectly good or worthy of worship and whose will should always be obeyed. But to do this he must have a moral criterion (a standard for what is morally good) that is independent of God's will or what people believe to be God's will. In fact, the believer's moral criterion— "because it is willed by God"—is logically dependent on some distinct criterion in virtue of which the believer judges that something is perfectly good and thus worthy of worship. And in making this very crucial judgment he cannot appeal to God's will as a criterion, for, that there is a being worthy of the appellation 'God', depends in part on the above prior moral claim. Only if it is correct can we justifiably say that there is a God.

It is crucial to keep in mind that 'a wholly good being exists who is worthy of worship' is not analytic—is not a truth of language—though 'God is wholly good' is. The former is rather a substantive moral statement (expressing a moral judgment) and a very fundamental one indeed, for the believer's whole faith rests on it. Drop this and everything goes.

It is tempting to reply to my above argument in this vein: "But it is blasphemy to judge God; no account of the logical structure of the believer's argument can be correct if it says that the believer must judge that God is good." Here we must beware of verbal magic and attend very carefully to precisely what it is we are saying. I did not—and could not on pain of contradiction—say that God must be judged worthy of worship, that he must be perfectly good; for God by definition is worthy of worship and is perfectly good. I said something quite different, namely, that the believer and the nonbeliever alike must decide whether there exists or could conceivably exist a force, a being ('ground of being') that is worthy of worship, or perfectly good; and I further said that in deciding this one makes a moral judgment that can in no way be logically dependent on God's will. Rather, the moral standard, 'because it is willed by God', is dependent for its validity on the acceptance of the claim that there is a being worthy of worship. And as our little word 'worthy' indicates, this is unequivocally a moral judgment for believer and nonbeliever alike.

There is a rather more baroque objection[11] to my argument that (a) nothing could count as the Judeo-Christian God unless that reality is worthy of worship and (b) it is our own moral insight that must tell us if anything at all is or ever possibly could be worthy of worship or whether there is a being who possesses perfect goodness. My conclusion from (a) and (b) was that rather than morality being based on religion, it can be seen that religion in a very fundamental sense must be based on morality. The counter-argument claims that such a conclusion is premature because the judgment that something is worthy of worship is not a moral judgment; it is an evaluative judgment, a religious evaluation, but not a moral judgment. The grounds for this counter-claim are that if the judgment is a moral judgment, as I assumed, then demonolatry—the worship of evil spirits—would be self-contradictory. But although demonolatry is morally and religiously perverse, it is not self-contradictory. Hence my argument must be mistaken.

However, if we say "Z is worthy of worship" or that, given Judeo-Christian attitudes, "If Z is what ought to be worshipped then Z must be good," it does not follow that demonolatry is self-contradictory or incoherent. Not everyone uses language as Jews and Christians do and not everyone shares the conventions of those religious groups. To say that nothing can be God, at least not the Judeo-Christian God, unless it is worthy of worship, and to affirm that the judgment of something as worthy of worship is a moral judgment, is not to deny that some people on some grounds could judge that what they believe to be evil spirits are worthy of worship. By definition, they could not be Jews or Christians—they show by their linguistic behavior that they do not believe in the Judeo-Christian God who, by definition, is perfectly good. Jews and Christians recognize that believers in demonolatry do not believe in God but in evil spirits whom such Joycean characters judge to be worthy of worship. The Christian and the demonolator make different moral judgments of a very fundamental sort reflecting different views of the world.

VI

The dialectic of our general argument about morality and divine commands should not end here. There are some further considerations that need to be brought to the forefront. Consider the theological claim that there is an infinite self-existent being upon whom all finite realities depend for their existence, but who in turn depends on nothing. Assuming the intelligibility of the key concepts in this claim and assuming also that we know this claim to be true, it still needs to be asked how we can know, except by the use of our own moral understanding, that this infinite, self-existent being is good or is a being whose commands we ought to obey. Since he—to talk about this being anthropomorphically by the use of the personal pronoun—is powerful enough, we might decide that it would be "the better part of valor" to obey him. But this decision would not at all entail that we ought to obey him. How do we know that this being is good, except by our own moral discernment? We could not discover that this being is good or just by discovering that he "laid the foundation of the world" or "created man in his image and likeness." No information about the behavior patterns of this being would of itself tell us that he was good, righteous, or just. We ourselves would have to decide that, or, to use the misleading idiom of the ethical intuitionist, we would have to intuit or somehow come to perceive or understand that the unique ethical properties of goodness, righteousness, and justness apply to this strange being or 'ground of all being' that we somehow discover to exist. Only if we independently knew what we would count as good, righteous, just, would we be in a position to know whether this being is good or whether his commands ought to be obeyed. That most Christians most of the time unquestionably assume that he is good only proves that this judgment is for them a fundamental moral judgment. But this should hardly be news.

At this point it is natural to reply: "Still, we would not even call this being God unless he was thought to be good. God, whatever else he may or may not be, is a fitting or proper object of worship." A person arguing thus might continue: "This is really a material mode statement about the use of the word 'God'; that is to say, we would not call Z God unless that Z were a fitting or proper object of worship or a being that ought to be worshipped. And if we say 'Z is a fitting object of worship' or 'Z ought to be worshipped' we must also be prepared to say 'Z is good.' Z could not be one without being the other; and if Z is a fitting object of worship, Z necessarily is a being we would call God. Thus, if Z is called God, then Z must also of necessity be called good since in Judeo-Christian contexts what ought to be worshipped must also be good. [This is a logical remark about the use of the phrase 'ought to be worshipped' in Judeo-Christian contexts.] God, by definition, is good. Though the word 'God' is not equivalent to the word 'good', we would not call a being or power 'God' unless that being was thought to be good."

The above point is well taken, but it still remains the case that the believer has not derived a moral claim from a non-moral religious one. Rather, he has only indicated that the word 'God', like the words 'Saint', 'Santa Claus', 'Hunky', 'Nigger', 'Mick', or 'Kike', is not a purely descriptive term. 'God', like 'Saint', etc., has an evaluative force; it expresses a pro-attitude on the part of the believer and does not just designate or even describe a necessary being or transcendent power or immanent force. Such a believer—unlike Schopenhauer—means by 'God' something toward which he has an appropriate pro-attitude; employing this word with its usual evaluative force, he could not say, "God commands it but it is really evil to do it." If, on the other hand, we simply think of what is purportedly designated or described by the word 'God'—the descriptive force of the word—we can say, for example, without paradox, "An objective power commands it but it is evil to do it." By simply considering the reality allegedly denoted by the word 'God', we cannot discover whether this 'reality' is good. If we simply let Z stand for this reality, we can always ask, "Is it good?" This is never a self-answering question in the way it is if we ask, "Is murder evil?" Take away the evaluative force of the word 'God' and you have no ground for claiming that it must be the case that God is good; to make this claim, with our admittedly fallible moral understanding, we must decide if this Z is good.

"But"—it will be countered—"you have missed the significance of the very point you have just made. As you say yourself, 'God' is not just a descriptive word and God-sentences are not by any means used with a purely descriptive aim. 'God' normally has an evaluative use and God-sentences have a directive force. You cannot begin to understand them if you do not take this into consideration. You cannot just consider what Z designates or purports to designate."

My reply to this is that we can and must if we are going to attain clarity in these matters. Certain crucial and basic sentences like 'God created the Heavens and the earth' and 'God is in Christ', are by no means just moral or practical utterances and they would not have the evaluative force they do if it were not thought that in some strange way they described a mysterious objective power. The religious quest is a quest to find a Z such that Z is worthy of worship. This being the case, the evaluative force of the words and of the utterance is dependent on the descriptive force. How else but by our own moral judgment that Z is a being worthy to be worshipped are we enabled to call this Z "my Lord and God"? Christians say there is a Z such that Z should be worshipped. Nonbelievers deny this or remain skeptical. Findlay,[12] for example, points out that his atheism is in part moral because he does not believe that there can possibly be a Z such that Z is a worthy object of worship. Father Copleston,[13] on the other hand, says there is a Z such that Z ought to be worshipped. This Z, Father Copleston claims, is a 'necessary being' whose nonexistence is in some important sense inconceivable. But both Findlay and Copleston are using their own moral understanding in making their respective moral judgments. Neither is deriving or deducing his moral judgment from the statement 'there is a Z' or from noticing or adverting to the fact—if it is a fact—that Z is 'being-itself', 'a reality whose nonexistence is unthinkable', 'the ground of being', or the like.

Morality cannot be based on religion. If anything, the opposite is partly true, for nothing can be God unless he or it is an object worthy of worship, and it is our own moral insight that must tell us if anything at all could possibly be worthy of worship.

It is true that if some Z is God, then, by definition, Z is an object worthy of worship. But this does not entail there is such a Z; that there is such a Z would depend both on what is the case and on what we, as individuals, judge to be worthy of worship. 'God is worthy of worship' is—for most uses of 'God'—analytic. To understand this sentence requires no insight at all but only a knowledge of English; but that there is or can be a Z such that Z is worthy of worship depends, in part at least, on the moral insight—or lack thereof—of that fallible creature that begins and ends in dust.

In her puzzling article, "Modern Moral Philosophy,"[14] Miss Anscombe has made a different sort of objection to the type of approach taken here. Moral uses of obligation statements, she argues, have no reasonable sense outside a divine-law conception of ethics. Without God, such conceptions are without sense. There was once a context, a religious way of life, in which these conceptions had a genuine application. 'Ought' was once equated, in the relevant context, with 'being obliged', 'bound', or 'required'. This came about because of the influence of the Torah. Because of the "dominance of Christianity for many centuries the concepts of being bound, permitted, or excused became deeply embedded in our language and thought."[15] But since this is no longer so unequivocally the case, these conceptions have become rootless. Shorn of this theistic Divine Law, shorn of the Hebrew-Christian tradition, these conceptions can only retain a "mere mesmeric force" and cannot be "inferred from anything whatever."[16] I think Miss Anscombe would say that I have shown nothing more than this in my above arguments. What I have said about the independence of morality from religion is quite correct for this "corrupt" age, where the basic principles of a divine-law conception of ethics appear merely as practical major premises on a par with the principle of utility and the like. In such contexts a moral 'ought' can only have a psychological force. Without God, it can have no "discernible content" for the conception of moral obligation "only operates in the context of law."[17] By such moves as I have made above, I have, in effect, indicated how moral obligation *now* has only a delusive appearance of content. And in claiming that without God there still can be genuine moral obligations I have manifested "a detestable desire to retain the atmosphere of the term 'morally obligatory' where the term itself no longer has a genuine use."[18] "Only if we believe in God as a law-giver can we come to believe that there is anything a man is categorically bound to do on pain of being a bad man."[19]

The concept of obligation has, without God, become a Holmes-less Watson. In our present context, Miss Anscombe argues, we should, if "psychologically possible," jettison the concepts of moral obligation, moral duty, and the like and approach ethics only after we have developed a philosophical psychology that will enable us to clarify what pleasure is, what a human action is, and what constitutes human virtue and a distinctively "human flourishing."[20]

I shall not be concerned here with the larger issues raised by Miss Anscombe's paradoxical, excessively obscure, yet strangely challenging remarks. I agree, of course, that philosophical psychology is important, but I am not convinced that we have not "done" ethics and cannot profitably "do" ethics without such a philosophical psychology. I shall, however, be concerned here only to point out that Miss Anscombe has not shown us that the notion of moral obligation is unintelligible or vacuous without God and his laws.

We have already seen that if so-and-so is called a divine command or an ordinance of God, then it is obviously something that the person who believes it to be a divine command or ordinance of God will believe he ought to obey, for he would not call anything a *divine* command or an ordinance of *God* unless he thought he ought to obey it. But we ourselves, by our own moral insight, must judge that such commands or promulgations are worthy of such an appellation. Yet no moral conceptions follow from a command or law as such. And this would be true at any time whatsoever. It is a logical and not a historical consideration.

Now it is true that if you believe in God in such a way as to accept God as your Lord and Master, and if you believe that something is an ordinance of God, then you ought to try to follow this ordinance. But if you behave like this, it is not because you base morals on religion or on a law concept of morality, but because he who can bring himself to say "my God" uses 'God' and cognate words evaluatively. To use such an expression is already to make a moral evaluation; the man expresses a decision that he is morally bound to do whatever God commands. 'I ought to do whatever this Z commands' is an expression of moral obligation. To believe in God, as we have already seen, involves the making of a certain value judgment;

that is to say, the believer believes that there is a Z such that Z is worthy of worship. But his value judgment cannot be derived from just examining Z, or from hearing Z's commands or laws. Without a pro-attitude on the part of the believer toward Z, without a decision by the individual concerned that Z is worthy of worship, nothing of a moral kind follows. But no decision of this sort is entailed by discoveries about Z or by finding out what Z commands or wishes. It is finally up to the individual to decide that this Z is worthy of worship, that this Z ought to be worshipped, that this Z ought to be called his Lord and Master. We have here a moral use of 'ought' that is logically prior to any law conception of ethics. The command gains obligatory force because it is judged worthy of obedience. If someone says, "I do not pretend to appraise God's laws, I just simply accept them because God tells me to," similar considerations obtain. This person judges that there is a Z that is a proper object of obedience. This expresses his own moral judgment, his own sense of what he is obliged to do.

A religious belief depends for its viability on our sense of good and bad—our own sense of worth—and not vice versa. It is crucial to an understanding of morality that this truth about the uses of our language be understood. Morality cannot be based on religion and I (like Findlay) would even go so far as to deny in the name of morality that any Z whatsoever could be an object or being worthy of worship. But whether or not I am correct in this last judgment, it remains the case that each person with his own finite and fallible moral awareness must make decisions of this sort for himself. This would be so whether he was in a Hebrew-Christian tradition or in a "corrupt" and "shallow" consequentialist tradition or in any tradition whatsoever. A moral understanding must be logically prior to any religious assent.

NOTES

1. Emil Brunner, *The Divine Imperative*, trans. Olive Wyon (London: Lutterworth Press, 1947), chapter 9.

2. P. H. Nowell-Smith, "Morality: Religious and Secular," in Ian Ramsey (ed.), *Christian Ethics and Contemporary Philosophy* (London: SCM Press, 1966).

3. A. C. Ewing, "The Autonomy of Ethics," in Ian Ramsey (ed.), *Prospect for Metaphysics* (London: Allen and Unwin, 1961).

4. Ibid., p. 39.

5. Ibid., p. 40.

6. Ibid., p. 4.

7. See D. A. Rees, "Metaphysical Schemes and Moral Principles," in *Prospect for Metaphysics*, op. cit., p. 23.

8. Ronald Hepburn, *Christianity and Paradox* (London: C. A. Watts, 1958), p. 132.

9. This is surely to assume a lot.

10. Finally we must be quite clear that X's being good is but a necessary condition for X's being the perfect good. But what would be a sufficient condition? Do we really know? I think we do not. We do not know how to identify the referent of 'the Perfect Good'. Thus in one clear sense we do not understand what such a phrase means.

11. This objection has been made in an unpublished paper by Professor T. P. Brown.

12. J. N. Findlay, "Can God's Existence be Disproved?" in Antony Flew and Alasdair MacIntyre (eds.), *New Essays in Philosophical Theology* (New York: Macmillan Company, 1955), pp. 47-56.

13. Bertrand Russell and F. C. Copleston, "The Existence of God: A Debate," in Bertrand Russell, *Why I am not a Christian* (London: Allen and Unwin, 1957), pp. 145-47.

14. Elizabeth Anscombe, "Modern Moral Philosophy," in *Philosophy* 33, no. 8 (January 1958).

15. Ibid., p. 5.

16. Ibid., p. 8.

17. Ibid., p. 18.

18. Ibid.

19. Ibid., p. 6.

20. Ibid., pp. 1, 15, 18

3

God and the Basis of Morality

I

Consider the fundamental religious beliefs common to the Judeo-Christian-Islamic traditions. If, as it seems likely, they cannot be proven to be true, can they be reasonably believed to be true because they can in some other way be justified? What I want to know is whether it is more reasonable to hold fundamental religious beliefs, such as there is a God and that we shall survive the death of our present bodies, than not to hold them. (I have discussed such general questions in Nielsen 1971a, 1971b, 1973a, and 1982a.)

Part of that probing, the whole of which is surely complicated and many faceted, will be the burden of this chapter. Here I shall put questions of immortality and bodily resurrection aside and only consider what is indeed even more central to Judaism and Christianity, namely, belief in God. It is—rightly or wrongly—widely believed now that no proof can be given of God's existence and that it is not even the case that we can give evidence or grounds for the claim that it is probable that God exists. Indeed, the very notion of trying to do any of these things is frequently thought to be a confusion based on a misconception of the realities of Jewish and Christian belief.

From *The Journal of Religious Ethics* 10, no. 2 (Fall 1982): 335-50.

(There are forceful statements of this in MacIntyre 1957 and 1959.) But it is also sometimes thought that such apologetic moves are entirely unnecessary, for, scandal to the intellect or not, a reasonable, morally concerned human being will accept God humbly on faith, for, without that faith and the belief in God which it entails, morality, human integrity, and the basis of our self-respect will be undermined and life will be revealed as an utterly useless passion. We must believe in God to make sense of our lives and to find a moral Archimedean point. Whatever intellectual impediments we have to belief in God, such a religious belief is morally necessary. Without it we can hardly have a rooted moral belief-system and without that, as social theorists such as Durkheim and Bell have stressed, we cannot have a stable, well-ordered society. I am not suggesting that the claim is, or should be, that we can 'will to believe' but I am asserting that the apologetic claim is that without belief people should conclude that a moral community is impossible and that life is indeed meaningless.

I shall argue that such an apologetic claim has not been sustained. There are, in my judgment, fundamental unresolved questions about the foundations of morality, and attempts, such as those of Mill, Kant, Sidgwick, and Rawls, to lay out a systematic moral philosophy to assess our moral practices and social institutions have not been remarkable for their success (Nielsen 1982b, 1982c). But such difficulties notwithstanding, there is no good ground for claiming that only through belief in God can we attain a sufficient moral anchorage to make sense of our tangled lives. I shall argue that there is some moral understanding that is *logically independent* of belief in God and is necessary even to be able to understand the concept of God and that, God or no God, some actions can be appreciated to be desirable and some as through and through evil and despicable. It is not true that if God is dead nothing matters. Belief in God cannot be justified, shown to be something we must just accept, if we are to be through and through reasonable, because it is a necessary foundation for the moral life. That, I shall argue, is just not so.

II

Let us first ask: "Is something good because God wills or commands it or does God command it because it is good?" If we say God commands it because it is good, this implies that something can be good independently of God. This is so because 'God commands it *because* it is good' implies that God apprehends it to be good or takes it to be good or in some way knows it to be good and then tells us to do it. But if God does this, then it is at least *logically* possible for us to come to see or in some way know or come to appreciate that it is good without God's telling us to do it or informing us that it is good. Moreover, on this alternative, its goodness does not depend on its being willed by God or even on there being a God.

The points made above need explanation and justification. In making those remarks, I am giving to understand that good is not a creation of God but rather that something is good is something which is itself apprehended by God or known by God. (If all that talk seems too "cognitive" a way to speak of moral notions, we can alternatively speak of God's appreciating something to be good.) If this is so, it is in some way there to be apprehended or known or appreciated and thus it is at least *logically* possible for us to apprehend it or know it or appreciate it without knowing anything of God. Furthermore, since God himself apprehends it to be good and since it doesn't, on this alternative, become good simply because he wills it or commands it, there can be this goodness even in a godless world. Translated into the concrete, this means that, at the very least, it could be correct to assert that even in a world without God, killing little children is evil and caring for them is good.

Someone might grant that there is this logical (conceptual) independence of morality from religion, but still argue that, given man's corrupt and vicious nature in his fallen state, he, as a matter of fact, needs God's help to understand what is good, to know what he ought to do, and to quite categorically bind himself to striving to act as morality requires.

Though there is indeed extensive corruption in the palace of justice, such a response is still confused. With or without a belief in God, we can recognize such corruption. In some concrete situations at least, we understand perfectly well what is good, what we ought to do, and what morality requires of us. Moreover, the corruption religious apologists have noted does not lie here. The corruption comes not principally in our knowledge or understanding but in our "weakness of will." We find it in our inability to do what in a cool hour, we acknowledge to be good—"the good I would do that I do not." Religion, for some people at any rate, may be of value in putting their *hearts* into virtue, but that religion is necessary for some in this way does not show us how it can provide us with a knowledge of good and evil or an ultimate criterion for making such judgments (Toulmin 1950: 202-225). It does not provide us, even if we are believers, with an ultimate standard of goodness.

Suppose we say instead—as Emil Brunner (1947) or C. F. Henry (1957), for example, surely would—that an action or attitude is right or good simply because God *wills* it or *commands* it. Its goodness arises from Divine *fiat*. God makes something good simply by commanding it.

Can *anything* be good or become good simply by being commanded or willed? Can a fiat, command, or ban *create* goodness or moral obligation? I do not think so. To see that it cannot, consider first some ordinary, mundane examples of ordering or commanding. Suppose I tell my students in a class I am teaching, "You must get a loose leaf notebook for this class." My commanding it, my telling my class they must do it, does not *eo ipso* make it something they *ought* to do or even make doing it good, though it might make it a prudent thing for them to do. But, whether or not it is prudent for them to do it, given my position of authority *vis-à-vis* them, it is, if there are no reasons for it, a perfectly arbitrary injunction on my part and not something that could correctly be said to be good.

Suppose, to use another example, a mother says to her college-age daughter, "It's not a good thing to go to school dressed like that." The mother telling her daughter that does not *eo ipso* make her daughter's manner of dress a bad thing. For her mother to be right here, she must be able to give reasons for her judgment that her daughter ought not to dress like that.

More generally speaking, the following are all perfectly intelligible:

(1) X wills y but should I do it?

(2) X commands it but is it good?

(3) X told me to do it, but all the same I ought not to do it.

(4) X proclaimed it, but all the same what he proclaimed is evil.

Statements (3) and (4) are not contradictions and (1) and (2) are not senseless, self-answering questions like 'Is a wife a married woman?' This clearly indicates that the moral concepts 'should', 'good', and 'ought' are not identified with the willing of something, the commanding or the proclaiming of something, or even with simply telling someone to do something. Even if moral utterances characteristically tell us to do something, not all "tellings to" are moral utterances. Among other things, "moral tellings to" are "tellings to" which, typically at least, must be supportable by *reasons*. This, however, is not true for simple commands or imperatives. In short, as a mere inspection of usage reveals, moral utterances are not identifiable with commands or anything of that order.

To this it will surely be replied: "It is true that these moral concepts cannot be identified with just any old command, but it is their being *Divine* commands which makes all the difference. It is *God's* willing it, *God's* telling us to do it, that makes it good" (Falk 1956: 123-131).

It is indeed true, for the believer at least, that it is *God's* commanding it or God's willing it that makes all the difference. This is so because the believer assumes and indeed fervently believes that God is good. But how, it should be asked, does the believer *know* that God is good, except by what is in the end his own quite fallible moral judgment or, if you will, appreciation or perception, that God is good? We must, to know that God is good, see that his acts, his revelation, his commands, are good. It is through the majesty and the goodness of his revelation, the depth and extent of his love, as revealed in the Scriptures, that we come to understand that God is good, that—so the claim goes—God is in reality the ultimate criterion for all our moral actions and attitudes.

It could, of course, be denied that *all* the commands, all the attitudes, exhibited in the Bible are of the highest moral quality. The behavior of Lot's daughters and the damnation of unbelievers are cases in point. But let us assume that the moral insights revealed in our Scriptures are of the very highest and that through his acts God reveals his goodness to us. But here we have in effect conceded the critical point put by the secularist. We can see from the very argumentation here that we must quite unavoidably use our own moral insight to decide that God's acts are good. We finally, and quite unavoidably, to come to any conclusion here, must judge for ourselves the moral quality of the alleged revelation; or, if you will, it is finally by what is no doubt fallible human insight that we must judge that what *purports* to be revelation is *indeed* revelation. We cannot avoid using our own moral understanding, corruptible and deceitful though it be, if we are ever to know that God is good. Fallible or not, our own moral understanding and judgment here is the *logically* prior thing.

The believer might indeed concede that if we start to inquire into, to deliberate about, the goodness of God, we cannot but end up saying what I have just said. But my mistake, he could argue, is in ever starting this line of inquiry in the first place. Who is man to inquire into, to question, the goodness of God? Who is he to ask whether God should be obeyed? That is utter blasphemy and folly. No *genuine believer* thinks for one moment he can question God's goodness or the bindingness of God's will. That God is good, that indeed God is the Perfect Good, is *a given* for the believer. 'God is good' or 'God is the perfect Good' are, in the technical jargon of philosophy, analytic. Given the believer's usage, it makes no sense to ask if what God commands is good or if God is good. Any being who was not good could not properly be called 'God', where what we are talking about is the God of the Judeo-Christian tradition. Similarly, we could not properly call anything that was not perfectly good God. A person who seriously queried "Should I do what God ordains?" could not possibly be a believer. Indeed, Jews and Christians do not mean by 'He should do x' that 'God ordains x'; and 'One should do what God ordains' is not equivalent to 'What God ordains God ordains'; but not all tautologies, or analytic propositions, are statements of identity. It is not only blasphemy, it is, as well, logically speaking *senseless to question* the goodness of God.

Whence then, one might ask, the ancient problem of evil? But let us, for the occasion, assume what it is at least reasonable to assume, namely, that in some way 'God is good' and 'God is the Perfect Good' are analytic or 'truths of reason'. Even if this is so, it still remains true—though now it is a little less easy to see this—that we can only come to know that anything is good or evil through our own moral insight.

Let us see how this is so. First it is important to see that 'God is good' is not an identity statement, e.g., 'God' is not equivalent to 'good'. "God spoke to Moses" makes sense. "Good spoke to Moses" is not even English. "The steak is good" and "Knowles's speech in Parliament was good" are both standard English sentences, but if 'God' replaced 'good' as the last word in these sentences we have gibberish. But, as I have just said, not all tautologies are statements of identity. 'Wives are women', 'Triangles are three-sided' are not statements of identity, but they are clear cases of analytic propositions. It is at least reasonable to argue 'God is good' has the same status, but, if it does, we still must independently understand what is meant by 'good' and thus the criterion of goodness remains *independent* of God.

As we could not apply the predicate 'women' to wives, if we did not first understand what women are, and the predicate 'three-sided' to triangles if we did not understand what it was for something to be three-sided, so we could not apply the predicate 'good' to God unless we already understood what it meant to say that something was good and unless we had some criterion of goodness. Furthermore, we can and do meaningfully apply the predicate 'good' to many things and attitudes that can be understood by a person who knows nothing of God. Even in a godless world, to relieve suffering would still be good.

But is not 'God is the Perfect Good' an identity statement? Do not 'God' and 'the Perfect Good' refer to and/or mean the same thing? The meaning of both of these terms is so very indefinite that it is hard to be sure, but it is plain enough that a believer cannot seriously question the truth of 'God is the Perfect Good' and still remain a Christian or Jewish believer. But granting that, we still must have a criterion for goodness that is independent of religion, that is, independent of a belief in God, for clearly we could not judge anything to be *perfectly* good unless we could judge that it was good, and we have already seen that our criterion for goodness must be at least logically independent of God.

Someone still might say: Something must have gone wrong somewhere. No believer thinks he can question or presume to *judge* God. A devoutly religious person simply must use God as his *ultimate criterion* for moral behavior (Brown 1963: 235-244, and 1966-67: 269-276, but in response see Nielsen 1971a: 243-257). If God wills it, he, as a "knight of faith," must do it!

Surely this is *in a way* so, but it is perfectly compatible with everything I have so far said. 'God' by *definition* is 'a being worthy of worship', 'wholly good', 'a being upon whom we are completely dependent'. These phrases partially define the God of Judaism and Christianity. This being so, it makes no sense at all to speak of *judging* God or deciding that God is good or worthy of worship. But the crucial point here is this: before we can make any judgments at all that any conceivable being, force, Ground of Being, transcendental reality, person or whatever could be *worthy* of worship, could be properly called 'good', let alone 'the Perfect Good', we must have a logically prior understanding of goodness (Nielsen 1964). That we could call anything, or any foundation of anything, 'God', presupposes we have a moral understanding and the ability to discern what would be *worthy* of worship or perfectly good. Morality does not presuppose religion; religion presupposes morality. Feuerbach was at least partially right: our very concept of God seems, in an essential part at least, a logical product of our moral categories. (For contemporary statements of this see Braithwaite 1964, and Hare 1973. See, in critical response, Nielsen 1981a.)

It is the failure to keep firmly in mind many of the distinctions that I have drawn above, some of which I also drew years ago in *Mind*, which makes it possible for D. Z. Phillips (1970: 223-233) to continue to claim that "nothing could be further from the truth" than to claim that "moral judgment is necessarily prior to religious assent" (Nielsen 1961: 175-186). It is not a question of "submitting God to moral judgment" but of the recognition that even to speak of a being or Being as being

God is already to have come to understand that that being is superlatively worthy of worship. This means that the person must have decided—using his own sense of good and evil—that there is some being who is worthy of worship and is properly called 'God' and thus is to be unconditionally obeyed. What Phillips fails to appreciate is that this very movement of thought and judgment shows that moral judgment is logically prior to religious assent. There is in short no recognition that something is worthy of worship without first recognizing that it is good.

It is worth noting that Phillips does nothing in his "God and Ought" (1970: 223-233) to show, against standard objections, how for believers, or for anyone else, " 'good' means 'whatever God wills'." A person with certain moral commitments—commitments about the worth of family relationships and the institution of the family—will pass from "He is my Father" to "I must not leave him destitute." But, as criticisms of Searle's attempted derivation of an ought from an is in effect show, the institutional facts appealed to are not themselves normatively neutral: they already embody certain moral commitments (Jaggar 1974, Nielsen 1978, Mackie 1977). Similarly a religious person will automatically go from "God wills it" to "I should do it," but he can do this only because he has already come to accept certain moral views in coming to believe *in* God. But that those distinctively religious normative views have not been enshrined, as logical or conceptual truths built into a language common to believer and nonbeliever alike, is shown in the fact that both believers and skeptics alike can intelligibly ask, as even Phillips admits, "Ought God's will be obeyed?"

Phillips also remarks that to "understand what it *means* to believe in God is to understand why God must be obeyed" (1970: 223-233). But this is plainly false, for one can very well understand what it is to believe in God and still not believe in God because one does not believe that there is, or perhaps even could be, anything *worthy* of worship, though, if one does believe in God—and does not just believe that there is an all-powerful and all-knowing being who created the world from nothing—one will also conclude that God must be obeyed. To believe in God is to accept an internal connection between the will of God and what one ought to do, but that is only possible for someone who comes to believe that there actually is a being *worthy* of worship who is to be called 'God', i.e., believes that this is to be his proper honorific title. Yet that very recognition, i.e., that there can be and indeed is a being worthy of worship, requires in a way that Phillips utterly misses, a moral judgment that is not logically dependent on any religious or theological understanding at all (1970: 223-233).

In *sum*, then, we can say this: a radically Reformationist ethic, divorcing itself from natural moral law conceptions, breaks down because something's being commanded cannot *eo ipso* make something good. Some Jews and Christians mistakenly think it can because they take God to be good and to be a being who always wills what is good. And it is probably true that 'God is good' has the status of a tautology or analyticity in Christian thought; still 'God is good' is not a statement of identity and we must first understand what 'good' means (including what criteria it has) before we can employ with understanding 'God is good' and 'God is Perfectly Good'. Moreover, we must be able to judge ourselves, concerning *any command* whatever, whether it ought to be obeyed; and we must use, whether we like it or not, our own moral insight and wisdom, defective though it undoubtedly is, to judge of anything whatsoever whether it is good. And if we are to avow such propositions at all, we cannot escape this for judgments about the Perfect Good. Indeed, with all our confusions and inadequacies, it is we human beings who finally must judge whether anything could *possibly* be so perfectly good or *worthy* of worship. If this be arrogance or Promethean hubris, it is inescapable, for such conceptual links are built into the logic of our language about God. We cannot base our morality on our conception of God. Rather our very ability to have the Jewish-Christian concept of God presupposes a reasonably sophisticated and independent moral understanding on our part. Brunner and Divine Command theorists like him have the whole *matter* topsy-turvy.[1]

III

Suppose someone argues that it is a matter of *faith* with him that what God commands is what he ought to do; it is a matter of *faith* with him that God's willing it is his ultimate criterion for something's being good. He might say, "I see the force of your argument, but for me it remains a straight matter of faith that there can be no goodness without God. I do not *know* that this is so; I cannot give *grounds* for believing that this is so; I simply humbly accept it on faith that something is good simply because God says that it is. I have no independent moral criterion."

My answer to such a fideist—to fix him with a label—is that in the very way he reasons, in his very talk of God as a being *worthy* of worship, he shows, his protestations to the contrary notwithstanding, that he has such an independent criterion. He shows in his very behavior, including his linguistic behavior, that something being willed or commanded does not *eo ipso* make it good or make it something that he ought to do, but that its being willed by a being *he takes* to be superlatively *worthy* of worship does make it something he, morally speaking, must do. But we should also note that it is by his own reflective decisions, by his own honest avowals, that he takes some being or, if you will, some x to be so *worthy* of worship, and thus he shows, in his very behavior, including his linguistic behavior, though not in his talk *about* his behavior, that he does not even take anything to be properly called 'God' unless he has already made a moral judgment about that being. He *says* that he takes God as his ultimate criterion for good on faith, but his actions, including, of course, his everyday linguistic behavior and not just his talk about talk, speak louder than his words, and he shows by them that even his God is in part a product of his moral awareness. Only if he had such a moral awareness could he use the word 'God', as a Jew or Christian uses it. So that his protestations notwithstanding, he clearly has a criterion for good and evil that is *logically independent* of his belief in God. His talk of faith does not and cannot at all alter that.

If the fideist replies: "Look, I take it on faith that your argument here or any such skeptical argument is wrong. I'll not trust you or any philosopher or even *my* own reason against *my* faith. I take my stand here on faith and I won't listen to anyone." If he takes his stand here, we must shift our argument. Whether he will listen or not, we can indeed point out that in so acting, he is acting like a blind, fanatical irrationalist— a man suffering from the systematic false consciousness of a *total* ideology.

Suppose he replies: "So what? Then I am an irrationalist!" We can then point out to him the painful consequences to himself and others of his irrationalism. We can point out to him that, even if, for some reason, he is right in claiming that one ought to accept a religious morality, he is mistaken in accepting it on such irrational grounds. The consequences of irrationalism are such that anything goes, and this, if really lived, would be disastrous for him and others. If he says, "So what; I do not even care about that," then it seems to me that, if we were to continue to reason with him, we would now have to, perhaps like a psychoanalytic sleuth, question his *motives* for responding in such a way. He can no longer have any reasons for his claims; we can only reasonably inquire into what *makes* him take this absurd stance.

There is another objection that I need briefly to consider. Someone might say: "I'm not so sure about all these fancy semantical arguments of yours. I confess I do not know exactly what to say to them, but one thing is certain, if there is a God, then he is the author, the creator, and the sustainer of everything. He created everything other than himself. Nothing else could exist without God and in this fundamental way morality and everything else is totally dependent on God. Without God there could be nothing to which moral principles or moral claims could be applied. Thus, in one important respect, morality, logic, and everything else are dependent on God."

I first would like to argue that there is a strict sense in which this claim of the religionist is not so. When we talk about what is morally good or morally right, we are not talking about what, except incidentally, is the case but about what ought to be the case or about what ought to exist. Even if there was nothing at all, that is, if there were no objects, processes, relations, or sentient creatures, it would still be correct to say that *if* there were sentient creatures, then a world in which there was less pain, suffering, degradation, and exploitation than there is in the present world would be a better world than a world such as ours. The truth of this is quite independent of the *actual* existence of either the world or of anything existing at all, though indeed we would have to have some *idea* of what it would be like for there to be sentient life and thus a world to understand such talk. Though no one could announce this truth if there were no people, and there would be no actual "we" or actual understanding of such talk, it still would be true that if there were such a country and it had a parliament, then it would be wrong to do certain things in it. It would be wrong to pass a law that allowed the exploitation of children or the torture of the innocent. To talk about what exists is one thing; to talk about what is good or about what ought to exist is another. God, let us assume, could, and indeed did, create the world, but he could not—logically could not—create moral values. Existence is one thing; value is another (Nielsen 1978). And it is no contravention of God's omnipotence to point out that he cannot do what is *logically* impossible.

If all this talk of what ought to be as being something independent of what is, is stuff of a too heady nature for you, consider this supplementary argument against the theist's reply. To assert that nothing would be good or bad, right or wrong, if nothing existed is not to deny that we can come to understand, without reference to God, that it is wrong to exploit underdeveloped countries and that religious tolerance is a good thing. The religious moralist has not shown that such exploitation would not be wrong and that such tolerance would not be good even if the atheist were right and God did not exist. But, if his position is to be made out, the religious apologist must show that in a godless world morality and moral values would be impossible. He must show that in such a world nothing could be good or bad or right or wrong. If there is no reason to believe that torturing little children would cease to be bad in a godless world, we have no reason to believe that, in any important sense, morality is dependent on religion. But God or no God, religion or no religion, it is still wrong to inflict pain on helpless infants when so inflicting pain on them is without any rational point (Ewing 1957: 49).

IV

There is a further stage in the dialectic of the argument about religion and ethics that I want now to consider. I have shown that in a purely logical sense moral notions cannot simply rest on the doctrinal cosmic claims of religion. In fact quite the reverse is the case, namely, that only if a human being has a concept of good and evil that is not religiously dependent can he even have the Jewish-Christian-Islamic conception of Deity? In this very fundamental sense, it is not morality that rests on religion but religion on morality. Note that this argument could be made out, even if we grant the theist his metaphysical claims about what there is. That is to say, the claims I have hitherto made are quite independent of skeptical arguments about the reliability or even the coherence of claims to the effect that God exists.

Some defenders of the faith will grant that there is indeed such a fundamental independence of ethical belief from religious belief, though very few would accept my last argument about the dependence of religious belief on human moral understanding. But what is important to see here is that they could accept at least part of my basic claim and still argue that to develop a *fully human and adequate normative* ethic one must make it a God-centered ethic (Hick 1959: 494-516). (For a criticism of such views see Nielsen 1973.) Here, in the arguments for and against, the intellectual reliability of religious claims will become relevant.

The claim that such a religious moralist wishes to make is that only with a God-centered morality could we get a morality that would be adequate, that would go beyond the relativities and formalisms of a nonreligious ethic. Only a God-centered and perhaps only a Christ-centered morality could meet our deepest and most persistent moral demands. People have certain desires and needs; they experience loneliness and despair; they create certain "images of excellence"; they seek happiness and love. If the human animal was not like this, if man were not this searching, anxiety-ridden creature with a thirst for happiness and with strong desires and aversions, there would be no good and evil, no morality at all. In short, our moralities are relative to our human natures. And given the human nature that we in fact have, we cannot be satisfied with any purely secular ethic. Nothing "the world" can give us will finally satisfy us. We thirst for a father who will protect us—who will not let life be just one damn thing after another until we die and rot; we long for a God who can offer us the promise of a blissful everlasting life with him. We need to love and obey such a father. Unless we can convincingly picture to ourselves that we are creatures of such a loving sovereign, our deepest moral hopes will be frustrated.

No purely secular ethic can—or indeed should—offer such a hope, a hope that is perhaps built on an illusion, but still a hope that is worth, the believer will claim, the full risk of faith. Whatever the rationality of such a faith, our very human nature, some Christian moralists maintain, makes us long for such assurances. Without it our lives will be without significance, without moral sense; morality finds its *psychologically realistic foundation* in certain human purposes. And given human beings with their nostalgia for the absolute, human life without God will be devoid of all purpose or at least devoid of everything but trivial purposes. Thus without a belief in God, there could be no humanly satisfying morality. Secular humanism in any of its many varieties is in reality inhuman.

It is true that a secular morality can offer no hope for a blissful immortality or a bodily resurrection to a "new life," and it is also true that secular morality does not provide for a protecting, loving father or some over-arching purpose *to* life. But we have to balance this off against the fact that these religious concepts are myths—sources of illusion and self-deception. We human beings are helpless, utterly dependent creatures for years and years. Because of this long period of infancy, there develops in us a deep psychological need for an all protecting father; we thirst for such security, but there is not the slightest reason to think that there is *such* security. Moreover, that people have feelings of dependence does not mean that there is something on which they can depend. That we have such needs most certainly does not give us any reason at all to think that there is such a super-mundane prop for our feelings of dependence.

Furthermore, and more importantly, if there is no such architectonic purpose *to* life, as our religions claim, this does not mean that there is no purpose *in* life—that there is no way of living that is ultimately satisfying and significant. It indeed appears to be true that all small purposes, if pursued too relentlessly and exclusively, leave us with a sense of emptiness.

Even Mozart quartets listened to endlessly become boring, but a varied life lived with verve and with a variety of conscious aims can survive the destruction of Valhalla. That there is no purpose *to* life does not imply that there is no purpose *in* life. Human beings may not have a function and if this is so, then, unlike a tape recorder or a pencil or even a kind of homunculus, we do not have a purpose. There is nothing we are made for. But even so, we can and do have purposes in the sense that we have aims, goals, and things we find worth seeking and admiring. There are indeed things we prize and admire; the achievement of these things and the realization of our aims and desires, including those we are most deeply committed to, give moral significance to our lives (Baier 1981; Nielsen 1981b). We do not need a God to *give* meaning to our lives by making us for his sovereign purpose and perhaps thereby robbing us of our freedom. We, by our deliberate acts and commitments, can give meaning to our own lives. Here man has that "dreadful freedom" that makes possible his human dignity; freedom will indeed bring him anxiety, but he will then be the *rider* and not the *ridden* and, by being able to choose, seek out, and sometimes realize those things he most deeply prizes and admires, his life will take on a significance (Berlin 1969). A life lived without purpose is indeed a most dreadful life—a life in which we might have what the existentialists rather pedantically call the experience of nothingness. But we do not need God or the gods to give purpose to our lives or to give the lie to this claim about nothingness. And we can grow into a fallibilism without a nostalgia for the absolute.

There are believers who would resist some of this and who would respond that these purely human purposes, forged in freedom and anguish, are not sufficient to meet our deepest moral needs. Beyond that, they argue, man needs very much to see himself as a creature with a purpose in a divinely ordered universe. He needs to find some *cosmic* significance for his ideals and commitments; he wants and needs the protection and certainty of having a function. This certainty, as the Grand Inquisitor realized, is even more desirable than his freedom. He wants and needs to live and be guided by the utterly sovereign will of God.

If, after wrestling through the kind of philosophical considerations I have been concerned to set forth, a religious moralist still really wants this and would continue to want it after repeated careful reflection, after all the consequences of his view and the alternatives had been placed vividly before him, after logical confusions had been dispelled, and after he had taken the matter to heart, his secularist interlocutor may find that with him he is finally caught in some ultimate disagreement in attitude.[2] Even this is far from certain, however, for it is not at all clear that there are certain determinate places in such dubious battles where argument and the giving of reasons just must come to an end and we must instead resort to persuasion or some other nonrational methods if we are to resolve our fundamental disagreements (Stevenson 1944: chapters 8, 9, and 13; Stevenson 1963: chapter 4; Stevenson 1966: 197-217).[3] But even if we finally do end up in such "pure disagreements in attitude," before we get there, there is a good bit that can be said. How could his purposes really be *his* own purposes, if he were a creature made to serve God's sovereign purpose and to live under the sovereign will of God? In such a circumstance would his ends be something he had deliberately chosen or would they simply be something that he could not help realizing? Moreover, is it really compatible with human dignity to be *made* for something? We should reflect here that we cannot without insulting people ask what they are for. Finally, is it not *infantile* to go on looking for some father, some order, some absolute, that will lift all the burden of *decision* from us (Evans 1973)? Children follow rules blindly, but do we want to be children all our lives? Is it really *hubris* or arrogance or sin on our part to wish for a life where we make our own decisions, where we follow the rules we do because we see the *point* of them, and where we need not crucify our intellects by believing in some transcendent purpose whose very intelligibility is seriously in question? Perhaps by saying this I am only exhibiting my own *hubris,* my own corruption of soul, but I cannot believe that to ask this question is to exhibit such arrogance.

NOTES

1. In reviewing the first edition of the present volume, Robert A. Oakes claims that 'God is good' is both analytic and substantive, whatever that could mean. Moreover, he believes that 'X is good' follows from 'God wills X'. "God's will," he tells us, "can be material of moral goodness without being constitutive of it." God's will "is to be taken as criterial of moral goodness precisely because 'a perfectly good being' is part of what is meant by 'God'." But this utterly fails to meet my argument that to even be able intelligibly to assert that there is a *perfectly* good being, we must have a logically prior criterion of what it is for something to be good. Thus, God's will cannot be our ultimate or most basic criterion of goodness. We must not only understand how to use 'good' before we can understand how to use 'God'; we must have some logically prior criterion of goodness or we could not know that there is a God, i.e., a perfectly good being worthy of worship or even understand what it is to make such a claim. It is not a dogma, or even a mistake, to claim that analytic propositions are nonsubstantive. There are no logically necessary genuine *existential* propositions, though there are propositions of a "there is" form that are logically necessary, e.g., "There is an infinite number of natural numbers," but, as Stuart Brown among others has shown against Norman Malcolm, there are very good grounds for believing that none of these statements are both existential and logically necessary (see Stuart Brown 1973: 33-40, and Robert A. Oakes 1975: 275). I should add that Oakes's account also misses the force of my arguments about appeals to God's will as being criterial of moral goodness (Nielsen, 1971a: 251-253).

2. That there is still a lot of room for argument here is brought out by Findlay (1963: chapters 4, 6, 9, and 15; and Findlay 1957: 97-114).

3. Even if, as thoroughly as Alasdair MacIntyre, we reject the "emotivism" of the "enlightenment project," we do not have a more objective basis for our moral claims if we follow MacIntyre's positive program (MacIntyre 1980 and 1981).

REFERENCES

Baier, Kurt. 1981. "The Meaning of Life," pp. 156-72 in E. D. Klemke (ed.), *The Meaning of Life*. New York: Oxford University Press.

Berlin, Isaiah. 1969. *Four Essays on Liberty*. New York: Oxford University Press.

Braithwaite, R. B. 1964. "An Empiricist's View of the Nature of Religious Belief," pp. 198-201 in John Hick (ed.), *The Existence of God*. New York: Macmillan.

Brown, Patterson. 1963. "Religious morality." *Mind* 72 (April): 235-44.

———. 1966. "God and the Good." *Religious Studies* 2, no. 2 (April): 269-76.

Brown, Stuart. 1973. *Proof and the Existence of God*. London: The Open University Press.

Brunner, Emil. 1947. *The Divine Imperative*. Trans. O. Wyon. Philadelphia: Westminister Press.

Evans, Donald. 1973. "Does Religious Faith Conflict with Moral Freedom?" pp. 305-42 in Gene Outka and John P. Reeder, Jr. (eds.), *Religion and Morality*. Garden City, N.Y.: Anchor Books.

Ewing, A. C. 1957. "The Autonomy of Ethics," pp. 62-83 in I. T. Ramsey (ed.), *Prospects for Metaphysics*. London: George Allen and Unwin.

Falk, W. D. 1956. "Moral Perplexity." *Ethics* 66 (January): 123-31.

Findlay, J. N. 1957. "The Structure of the Kingdom of Ends." *Proceedings of the British Academy* 43: 97-114.

———. 1963. *Language, Mind and Value*. London: George Allen and Unwin.

Hare, R. M. 1973. "The Simple Believer," pp. 294-304 in Gene Outka and John P. Reeder, Jr. (eds.), *Religion and Morality*. Garden City, N.Y.: Anchor Books.

Henry, F. H. 1957. *Christian Personal Ethics*. Grand Rapids, Mich.: William B. Eardmans.

Hick, John. 1959. "Belief and Life: The Fundamental Nature of the Christian Ethic." *Encounter* 20, no. 4 (January): 494-516.

Jaggar, Alison. 1974. "It Does Not Matter Whether We Can Derive 'Ought' from 'Is'." *Canadian Journal of Philosophy* 3, no. 3 (March): 373-79.

MacIntyre, Alasdair. 1957. "The Logical Status of Religious Belief," pp. 169-205 in Ronald Hepburn, Alasdair MacIntyre, and Stephen Toulmin (eds.), *Metaphysical Beliefs*. London: S. C. M. Press.

———. 1959. *Difficulties in Christian Belief*. London: SCM Press.

———. 1980. "A Crisis in Moral Philosophy: Why Is the Search for the Foundations of Ethics so Frustrating?" pp. 18-35 in H. T. Engelhardt, Jr. and Daniel Callahan (eds.), *Knowing and Valuing*. Volume IV, *The Foundations of Ethics and Its Relationship to Science*. Hastings-on-Hudson, N.Y.: The Hastings Center.

———. 1981. *After Virtue*. Notre Dame, Ind.: University of Notre Dame Press.

Mackie, John. 1977. *Ethics: Inventing Right and Wrong*. Harmondsworth, Middlesex, England: Penguin Books.

Nielsen, Kai. 1961. "Some Remarks on the Independence of Morality from Religion." *Mind* 70 (April): 175-86.

———. 1964. "God and the Good: Does Morality Need Religion?" *Theology Today* 211 (April): 47-58.

———. 1971a. *Reason and Practice*. New York: Harper and Row.

———. 1971b. *Contemporary Critiques of Religion*. New York: Herder and Herder.

———. 1973a. *Skepticism*. New York: St. Martins Press.

———. 1973b. *Ethics Without God*. London: Pemberton Books; Buffalo, N.Y.: Prometheus Books.

———. 1978. "Why There Is a Problem About Ethics." *Danish Yearbook of Philosophy* 15: 68-96.

———. 1981a. "Christian Empiricism." *The Journal of Religion* 61, no. 2 (April): 146-67.

———. 1981b. "Linguistic Philosophy and the Meaning of Life," pp. 175-92 in E. D. Klemke (ed.), *The Meaning of Life*. New York: Oxford University Press.

———. 1982a. *An Introduction to the Philosophy of Religion*. London: The Macmillan Press Ltd.

———. 1982b. "On Needing a Moral Theory." *Metaphilosophy* 13 (April): 36-45.

Nielsen, Kai. 1982c. "Grounding Rights and a Method of Reflective Equilibrium." *Inquiry* 25: 1–30.

Oakes, Robert A. 1975. "Review of *Ethics Without God.*" *Philosophy and Phenomenological Research* 361 (December): 273-76.

Phillips, D. Z. 1970. *Faith and Philosophical Enquiry.* London: Routledge and Kegan Paul.

Stevenson, C. L. 1944. *Ethics and Language.* New Haven: Yale University Press.

———. 1963. *Facts and Values.* New Haven: Yale University Press.

———. 1973. "Ethical Fallibility," pp. 197-217 in Richard T. DeGeorge (ed.), *Ethics and Society.* Garden City, N.Y.: Anchor Books.

Toulmin, Stephen. 1950. *An Examination of the Place of Reason in Ethics.* Cambridge, England: Cambridge University Press.

4

Religious versus Secular Morality

I

In chapter two, I attempted to develop and defend what is, in its essentials, an argument first set forth by Plato in his *Euthyphro*. It is an argument designed to establish that a morality, even a religious morality, cannot simply be based on a belief in God. That God ordains or wills certain things cannot be the ultimate ground for our moral assent.

It may be prudent to do what a powerful being—a Hitler or a Stalin, for example—commands, but this certainly does not make the doing of it morally obligatory. It does not by itself even constitute a relevant moral reason for doing it. For 'God commanded it' to be a morally relevant reason for doing something, let alone a definitive moral reason for doing it, it must, at least, be the case that God is good. A believer, of course, believes this to be the case, but what grounds does he have for this belief? If he says that he knows this to be true because the record of the Bible, the state of the world or the behavior of Jesus displays God's goodness, the believer himself clearly displays by his very response that he has some logically prior criterion for moral belief that is not based on the fact that there is a deity.

Yet it is more natural for a believer to reject the very question "How do you know God is good?" on the grounds that it is senseless. It is like asking "How do you know that scarlet things are red?" or "How do you know that puppies are young?" If he is something of a philosopher, he might tell you that " 'God is good,' like 'puppies are young,' is analytic, it is a truth of language. We could not—logically could not—call any being, ground of being, power or force 'God' if we were not also prepared to attribute or ascribe goodness to it." This is indeed so. As we can only call the dog we see in the park a puppy, if we already understand 'young' and know how to judge whether or not a dog is young, so we can properly call some being, force, or power 'God' only if we already know how to judge whether or not such a being, force, or power is good. In this fundamental way even the devout religious believer cannot possibly base his morality on his religion—that is, on his belief in God. He, too, has an even more fundamental criterion for judging something to be good or morally obligatory. Since this is so, God cannot be the only criterion for moral belief, let alone the only fundamental or adequate moral criterion. We must look elsewhere for the foundations of morality.

A defender of Judeo-Christian ethics could accept this and still maintain that there could be no adequate or genuine morality without God. He might say that though we must have some understanding of good and we must have some criteria for moral terms that are not derived from our religion, it remains the case that only a God-centered morality could satisfy our most persistent moral demands.

How could religious moralists defend such a claim? They could start by arguing that I have considered the question of morality and religion in too rarefied an atmosphere. I have treated morality as if it were in a vacuum. I have failed to take into consideration the enormous importance to morality of questions concerning man's human nature (his actual desires and needs) and the concrete nature of the world he lives in. Indeed, we cannot derive what we ought to do from any statements that merely assert that so and so is the case; but in deciding what to make the case, in deciding what is worth seeking, what is ultimately desirable, we most surely need to have some clear understanding of what is the case. Such an understanding is something to which any sane morality aspires.

Any realistic morality—secular or religious—links in some close way with what men on reflection actually desire and with that illusive thing we call human happiness. Such moralists would be in fundamental agreement with Nowell-Smith's remark that "if men had no desires and aversions, if they felt no joy and no remorse, if they were totally indifferent to everything in the universe, there would be no such thing as choice and we should have no concept of morality, of good and evil."[1]

We surely cannot crudely identify 'good' with 'object of desire', yet if men did not have certain desires and aversions, certain wants and needs, there would be no morality at all.

Such moralists could then point out that philosophers as different as Aristotle and Mill have wanted to say something more than this: we indeed seek many things and have many desires, yet all are but particular expressions of a more general desire. A man may want a civic office, a well-heeled wife, the ownership of a newspaper, a trusteeship in a university, but he wants these things because they are means to power and prestige. He, in turn, craves power and prestige because he is seeking security. He seeks security because only through attaining security can he attain what all men desire, namely, human happiness. And it is at just this juncture that the religious moralist can attack the purely secular moralist. He will meet the secularist on his own ground and argue that the secular moralist's great mistake *is in failing to see that in God alone can man find lasting happiness—the goal of all moral striving.*[2]

John Hick defends such a view in his essay "Belief and Life: The Fundamental Nature of the Christian Ethic."[3] It is also defended in a similar manner by Alasdair MacIntyre in his *Difficulties in Christian Belief.*[4] Following Aristotle and Mill, they claim that our basic desire is the desire for happiness: it is the ultimate goal for all human beings. They recognize that to make this claim is not to assert a grand anthropological hypothesis. Hick makes it quite explicit that his statement has the status of an implicit definition. Yet he claims that this does not make the identification of the final object of human desire trivial.

Christian philosophers such as Professor Hick take yet another step with Aristotle. While not sharing Aristotle's particular conception of the content of human happiness or lasting contentment, they do share his overall semantic requirement that we identify human happiness with whatever it is that we humans desire simply for its own sake and never simply as a means to anything else. That is, they agree, that Aristotle was right in claiming that "happiness is that which mankind desires above all else." We seek this or that specific objective because we rightly or wrongly believe that its attainment will minister to our happiness.

The question as to what will and what will not make us happy or contribute to our happiness is a factual question. The correct answer will depend on what men are like and how the world goes. Aristotle (as well as Plato) thought that the happiness of any kind of creature consisted in the fulfillment of its own *telos* or purpose, that is, in the realization of its own end. The happiness of a human being must accordingly consist in the fulfillment of what it is that makes a man a man. In Cardinal Mercier's phrase, it consists in the achievement of "man's rational nature." If we realize our distinctively human potentialities, we will attain happiness; if not, we will not.

If we have a firm faith in God, these religious moralists argue, and if we have some understanding of what he wishes for us, we can come to see that man's purpose is very different from what a man with secular knowledge alone would take to be man's purpose. In fact, in a very real sense, God is the sustainer or custodian of our values, for without him, our lives would have no purpose. Even if 'good' cannot be defined as 'what God wills', knowledge of the reality revealed in the Jewish and Christian creeds makes it plain that man lives not for himself alone but was created by God for fellowship with Him. Man's purpose involves the love and acknowledgment of God. To love God is the fundamental reason for man's existence. If the fulfilling of one's nature is in harmony with the determining realities of one's total environment, such a fulfilment will bring happiness. If we accept the creeds of Judaism and Christianity, we believe that the "divine purpose of man is destined to final fruition." We *trust* that the universe is not such as to finally frustrate man's efforts to fulfill his purpose and to attain not only happiness but eternal bliss. If we come to know God, we must also come to regard him as a good shepherd who will protect his children and guide their lives according to his own good purpose.

A recognition of this fact about our world will free man from anxiety. Our attitude toward life will, in some significant respects, be like the attitude of a very small child whose parents unambivalently love him. The child's sense of being securely loved is a major psychological device in giving him a sense of peace, warmth, and stability. Similarly, "the knight of faith" will, Hick argues, manifest the "fruit of the spirit," which is "love, joy, peace, patience, kindness, goodness, faithfulness, gentleness, self-control." If our faith could be like a child's, we could live with this inner contentment and give uncalculatingly to others; but Hick, like Niebuhr, is aware that since "the fall" the ambivalent, tortured creature we call "the human animal" cannot attain this blissful state. Nonetheless, he can sometimes approximate it, and the closer he comes to this, the closer he comes to attaining genuine happiness.

II

However, it is on these very contested gounds concerning human happiness and the ends of life that religious morality has a competitor in secular morality. Many secular moralists see that the overall rationale of moral rules is linked to achieving the maximum in human happiness and the minimum in human suffering for all the people involved. Against such a secular conception of morality, a religious moralist must make good his claim that secular moralities, like utilitarianism, lack a real understanding of what happiness is. They lack the awareness of a transcendent Divine Purpose that gives man the supreme gift of blessedness, whose full glory transcends our imaginations. As the Scottish Shorter Catechism puts it, "Man's chief end is to glorify God and enjoy Him for ever and ever." Man's fullest happiness, man's distinctive flourishing, consists in the attainment of this state.

It may indeed be true, the religious moralist will continue, that we cannot determine what is good or what we ought to do from a knowledge that there is a deity and that He issues certain commands. In that sense Plato is right and morality is independent of religion; but in another deeper, more important sense, morality is dependent on religion. The above remarks about happiness and man's purpose should make this 'deeper sense' reasonably clear. Understanding what morality is all about, secularists and religious people alike know that morality is integrally connected with human happiness. But the man of faith alone realizes that man, with his deep and pervasive longing for immortality, can find "lasting and supreme happiness" only in God. As St. Augustine says: "Our hearts are restless until they find rest in Thee." Without God, life is just one damn thing after another, without our ever knowing what we want or why we want it. Without a belief in God—a Sovereign Lord—who loves us, promises us protection and finally the bliss of immortality, our lives must remain impoverished. Inner peace and contentment can come only through a belief in God.

Secular ethics, it is argued, also links morality with human desires and needs, but the picture of human happiness it gives us is, at best, superficial. Missing the dark insights of Pascal and Kierkegaard, secular ethics exhibits no deep understanding of the innermost wishes, fears, anxieties, or hopes of the human animal. But a religiously backed morality does understand that without God man's deepest wishes cannot be gratified. Without God, man will despair and will not attain the deepest, truest form of human happiness.

It is not only true that man will despair without God, but if we are aware of the reality of God, we will come to see that many of the things we would otherwise rationally desire are not really worth having. Like Hesse's Siddhartha, we will undergo a radical transformation. We will come to see that many of our hopes are vain and that the possibility of realizing other deeper, more lasting, desires becomes a reality for us when we come to know the reality of God. What it s rational to do, and what constitutes a reasonable wish, depends on the environment in which we live. The recognition of the truth, or even the meaningfulness of certain creedal or doctrinal statements, makes it rational to seek certain things that it would otherwise be irrational to seek. If, for example, we accept the creedal and doctrinal statements of Christianity, the moral teachings of this religion become rational, while without the creed and the doctrine, the moral code is "absurdly quixotic and impractical."

In this way the Christian ethic is based on Christian beliefs about the nature of God and his relation to man. If we understand them we can understand the point of doing some things that would otherwise seem very foolish. As Niebuhr has said, the

Christian ethic is not an ethic that squares with our secular understanding of what we ought to do. In accepting the Christian ethic or, for that matter, any religious ethic, we are not just accepting a set of commands; beyond that we are freely adopting a way of life that will radically transform our aims in life. And the way of life depicted in Jesus' teachings directs us voluntarily to relinquish much that we would ordinarily prize. We are asked to give up wealth, power and the approval of one's peers. Christian morality, as any religious morality, is a way of life that aims, in general, not at promoting the agent's own interests, as these are usually identified, but rather at serving his neighbors in their various needs. While it need not be an ascetic or "world-renouncing" ethic, the Christian ethic is a markedly other-regarding ethic. It requires sacrifices of human beings and it requires them to put aside what, from a purely secular point of view, they would take to be in their own rational interest. But it also claims that human beings will only achieve lasting human happiness if they so act.

God supplies us with the motive for acting in what, from a secular point of view, seems to be a very odd way. It is Professor Hick's contention that once we come to really know God, once we come to know what he is like and why he has created us, then we will freely decide to live in a way radically different from the one we would choose if we did not know our redeemer. In fact, if we really know God, we must love him. 'Knowing' here is not just an acquaintance with a certain experience or the acknowledgment that a certain statement is true: to know "God as Lord and Father is to live in a certain way, which is determined by the character and purposes of God."[5] To be aware of God is to see the world from a different slant and to react differently to it. (That does not mean that such awareness is only to see the world from such a slant.) Given this specifically religious awareness, many policies and aims that would otherwise be unreasonable become highly reasonable and desirable aims or policies. Given a proper understanding of the nature of reality, the seemingly unpractical nature of the Christian and Jewish codes will now be seen to be highly practical—indeed they square with what a rational man would desire. Given such a new understanding of the world, we see what genuine happiness is and how it is utterly dependent on God. As Hick puts it:

Jesus' teaching does not command that we live in a way which runs counter to our deepest desires, and which would thus require some extraordinary counterbalancing inducement. Rather, he reveals to us the true nature of the world in which we are living and indicates in the light of this the only way in which our deepest desires can be fulfilled. In an important sense, then, Jesus does not propose any new motive for action. He does not set up a new end to be sought, or provide a new impulse to seek an already familiar end. Instead, he offers a new vision, or mode of appreciation of the world, such that to live humanely in the world as it is thus seen to be, is to live the kind of life which Jesus describes. The various attitudes and policies for living which he sought to replace are expressions of a sense of insecurity which is natural enough if the world really is, as most people take it to be, an arena of competing interests in which each must safeguard himself and his own against the rival egoisms of his neighbors. If human life is essentially a form of animal life, and human civilization a refined jungle in which self-concern operates more subtly but not less surely than by animal tooth and claw, then the quest for invulnerability in its many guises is entirely rational. To seek security in the form of power over others, whether physical, psychological, economic, or political, or in the form of recognition and acclaim would then be indicated by the character of our environment. But Jesus rejects these attitudes and objectives as based upon an estimate of the world which is false because it is atheistic; it assumes that there is no God, or at least none such as Jesus knew. Jesus was accordingly far from being an idealist, if by this we mean one who sets up ideals and recommends us to be guided by them instead of by the realities around us. He was a realist presenting a life in which the neighbor is valued equally with the self as indicated by the character of the universe as it really is. He urged men to live in terms of reality; and his morality differs from the normal morality of the world because his view of reality differs from the normal view of the world. . . . The universe is so constituted that to live in it in the manner which Jesus has described is to build one's life upon enduring foundations, whilst to live in the opposite way is to go "against the grain" of things and to court ultimate disaster. Jesus assumes that as rational beings we want to live in terms of reality, and he is concerned to tell us what the true structure of reality is.[6]

III

What are we to say to Hick? One thing is quite plain—and here I am in agreement with Professor Hick: if the creedal and doctrinal claims of Judaism or Christianity were true, then it would indeed be rational to act as Hick's believer is convinced we ought to act. We cannot deduce moral statements from factual ones but we all repeatedly and typically use factual statements to back up our moral statements. The effects of air pollution on health and of population growth on the environment are clearly relevant to the choices human beings should make about technological development and population growth. That Jones habitually has several lovers and regularly drinks himself into a stupor is patently relevant to Frannie's decision that she ought not to marry him. A person who knowingly ignores such factual considerations in making moral decisions behaves irrationally. A "knight of the absurd" who utterly ignores the relevant facts in coming to moral decisions is a man who clearly belongs in an insane asylum.

So far, I agree with Hick. We should make our moral judgments in the light of what the facts are. But it is just Hick's account of the facts that seems to me to be so totally unrealistic, so devoid of a genuine sense of reality. In critically considering his account, all the old, as well as some new, objections to religion come trooping back in. We have no evidence at all for believing in the existence or love of God. None of the proofs works; we (or some of us, at any rate) have religious experiences, but these religious experiences do not establish, even with any probability, that there is an unlimited being, a transcendent cause of the universe. These experiences can always be interpreted naturalistically or nontheistically. There is no logical bridge from these experiences to God.[7] Worse still, the very meaning of the term 'God' is opaque. We say "God is distinct from the universe and the creator of the universe," but we have no idea of what we would have to encounter now or hereafter to encounter a transcendent cause or a creator of the universe. If we speak, as Father Bochenski has,[8] of "supernatural perceptions," we are (to put it mildly) 'explaining' the obscure by the still more obscure. The plain fact is that we do not have any grounds for believing that God exists or for believing that his purposes are good; and our troubles are compounded when we realize that we do not even know what we would have to experience for it to be true or even probable that God exists, or that God loves man. That this is so raises, as Professor Hick is keenly aware, serious questions about the very intelligibility of such utterances. It will do no good to say "We now see as through a darkened glass but hereafter we shall see face-to-face," for, even if man is immortal, if we do not now know what it would be like to verify the statements 'God exists' and 'God loves us', the simple fact that we some day may wake up on "the other shore" will not help us to verify that there is a God. Immortality is possible even in a Godless universe.

Hick, as part of a good Protestant tradition, might welcome such an answer by saying that unless we are in "the circle of faith," we cannot even understand these matters. But this reply will not do, for while we might take it on faith that God exists, in lieu of having evidence for his existence, we cannot take the intelligibility of 'God exists' or 'God shall raise the quick and the dead' utterly on faith, for we must first understand *what* it is we are to take on faith.[9] But even if we were able to appeal to faith here, we are still faced with the quite elementary and yet quite staggering anthropological fact that there are thousands of religions with conflicting revelations, most of them claiming ultimate authority and ultimate truth in matters of religion. Which one are we to choose? Why should we think, as finite men, historically and ethnically bound, that our religion and our tribe alone should have the one true revelation? We are members of one historically bound culture on a minor planet in an unbelievably vast universe. Why should it be that in these matters we have a unique hold on the truth? To think that we do is to have a fantastically unrealistic picture of the world.

If we say, by way of rebuttal, that in talking about religion we should only consider the great or the higher religions, we run into a host of difficulties. First, these religions often differ very radically from each other. Consider, for example, Judaism and Thervada Buddhism. Furthermore, the laudatory labels 'great' and 'higher' are question-begging. Do we decide they are higher by an appeal to our own faith or our own revelation? If we do, we move in a very small and vicious circle. Do we decide they are higher or great religions because they have more members or cover geographically wider areas? If we do, why should such considerations be taken as relevant reasons for such a judgment? Certainly we do not use such criteria in judging which cultures have the most advanced forms of music, dance or science. Such an appeal in religion is quite arbitrary. If we say that we call these religions higher because they exhibit a deeper moral insight into man's condition, then we have used—as I think we often do in practice—our own quite secular moral understanding to judge religions and we clearly indicate that we do not need these religions to back up our morality. (Viewed in this way, Christianity and Judaism do not seem to me to come off as spectacular successes.)

In short, there is not the slightest reason to believe that the Christian is living according to 'the reality principle' while the non-Christian, and the secularist in particular, is deluded about man's true estate. Christianity is myth-eaten. The very intelligibility of the key concepts of the religion is seriously in question; there is no evidence whatsoever for the existence of God; and when we keep an anthropological perspective in mind, we will come to recognize that the revelation and authority of Christianity are but one revelation and one authority among thousands of conflicting revelations and authorities. Given this state of affairs, it is the epitome of self-delusion to believe that Jesus really reveals what the true structure of reality is.

IV

Those in the tradition of Kierkegaard are likely to assert here that I have missed the deepest appeal of Christianity. Certainly God, Christ, and religion in general are absurd; Christianity is surely a genuine scandal to the intellect, but we need it all the same, for, as Camus and Sartre recognize, man's very condition in this world is absurd and if there is no God, man's life must be meaningless—a stupid game of charades, without any rationale at all. It is true, as Luther said, that if a man is to be a sound-believing Christian, he must tear out the eyes of his reason, but unless he does this, unless—indeed in utter darkness—he makes the leap of faith, he will never attain lasting happiness. Without a belief in God, he will be driven to despair.

This is so because man can only find lasting happiness in God. This is why, in spite of all the intellectual and emotional impediments to belief, one should join the circle of faith.

In all sobriety, what we need to ask is this: is there good sociological or psychological evidence to show that people will despair, will lose their sense of identity and purpose if they do not become followers of Christ? There are cultures, cultures that have never even heard of Christianity, let alone adopted it, that have, as far as we can tell, members who are just as happy and live with just as much a sense of purpose as we do. This shows that it is not true that we can save ourselves from despair only by following Christ. The burden of proof is surely on the Christian to show that the Christian faith alone saves man from despair and gives orientation and point to his life.

Perhaps what is being claimed is the more general thesis that without a belief in God, man will be driven to despair. Neither Judaism nor Christianity need be taken to be essential. But belief in divine providence is essential.

However, while it is true that there are people whose lives would lose all direction if they lost their God, it is also true that there are nonbelievers who have lived happy and productive lives, people such as John Dewey, George Eliot, and George Bernard Shaw. To this it is natural to reply: "Well, that may work for intellectuals, for some severely reflective men who will not draw warmth from the tribal campfire, but it will never work for the plain man." But it has. Chinese civilization, for example, or that part of it under the sway of Confucianism, has a religion that, for all practical purposes, is Godless, yet Confucianists have continued to live purposeful lives.

It is interesting to note that when such arguments for the necessity of faith are made by religious apologists, they do not, as a rule, put such a contention to empirical test, but assert, after the fashion of Kierkegaard, that a man *must* despair without God. The nonbeliever who does not show despair is really a man who suffers from some "hidden perturbation"— some deep but disguised estrangement from his true being. While this may be true of some nonbelievers, it remains for the believer to show that there is in all nonbelievers some such disquietude. (They might start by considering the lives of Bentham, Freud, and Dewey.) We need evidence here and not just *a priori dicta* that man must despair without God or that man will be happier with a belief in God. Moreover, it should be shown that man needs not just an undifferentiated theism, but also the concrete specifications of a living theistic religion. Thus we are led back to Judaism and Christianity.

Pascal shows in his *Pensées* that with Christ man has the hope of redemption and eternal bliss that the secularist does not have; but with the Jewish and Christian religions, one also has a sense of sin and unworthiness that, as in the case of Stephan Daedalus in *The Portrait of The Artist as a Young Man,* or Jerome in *La Porte Etroite,* can drive one to self-loathing and despair. If it is replied that since The Fall we have been tormented and that the "old Adam" is in us all—even after Christ came to redeem us—then what grounds have we for claiming that people within Christianity will be happier than people outside the "circle of faith"?

Generally speaking, believers are neither happier nor are they better adjusted than nonbelievers. There are sick, paranoid, and vile believers and there are sick, paranoid, and vile nonbelievers; there are sane, humane, and happy believers, and there are sane, humane, and happy nonbelievers. Personal virtue and vice seem to be completely independent of doctrinal affiliation.

Not many (if any) religious apologists wish to make this issue an empirical, anthropological issue. They have a certain picture of life, and reasoning in accordance with this picture they conclude that man must despair without God. Secular moralists, they argue, can have no real understanding of what human happiness is. Here we have a purely *a priori* philosophical argument. But is it a good one? I think not. In the first place, the religionist frequently depicts a secularist morality in ·a way—as Hick does—that makes it seem egoistic and a kind of gross hedonism in which man is nothing more than a purely self-concerned, clever little animal.[10] We come to picture secular moralities as committing us to a vision of the good life that consists in devotion to pleasures like those gained from taking Turkish baths and watching belly dancers. But no secularist need deny the dignity of man nor devote himself exclusively, or at all, to such pleasures. Once we rid ourselves of such stereotypes, why should we say that the believer alone knows what "true happiness" is?

At this point, Hick and other theologians, both Protestant and Catholic, trot out a very ancient argument—an argument that in essence goes back to Plato and Aristotle. The happiness of a human being must consist in the fulfillment of what it is that makes a man a man. Only when he achieves what it is that he was "cut out to be" will he achieve lasting contentment. But the believer alone knows what man was cut out to be, so he alone can know the nature of true happiness and thus of true virtue. (That is a slippery 'thus' but we shall let it pass.)

But why should we assume that man was cut out to be anything, that he has some function that he must realize if he is not to suffer alienation? Man has certain distinctive capabilities: he can reason, that is, he can use symbols; he is permanently sexed; he alone laughs; he is the only animal to suffer anxiety and fear death. But why does he realize himself more adequately by developing any or all of those capacities? Perhaps he would be happier, for example, if he were less intellectual. And how can we show that he was cut out for anything? Policemen, teachers, thieves, bar-maids, janitors, and barbers have certain roles, certain more or less distinctive functions. So do husbands, suitors, fathers, and daughters. All of us have diverse social roles—roles that frequently conflict. But what is our role or function *qua* human being? While firemen have a clear function, man does not. The question 'What are people made for?' has no clear meaning in the way that 'What are customs officers for?' does. And to say that men were made to worship and love God is completely question-begging. It seems to me that man was not made for anything.[11]

The inevitable counter is that if man was not made for something, if there is not something he was cut out to be, human living will be a nihilistic nightmare, for man's life will then be totally without purpose or point. If God did not create man for some end, there can be no purpose to human living. It is when we see this—it is just when we see and take to heart the fact that without God life would be as Hardy and Schopenhauer depict it—that we are driven to God. We will then realize, as Tolstoy came to, that without God our lives will be without a purpose, without a rationale.

V

There is a plethora of confusion in such apologetics. It is indeed true that a purposeless life is a horrible life, a life that no sane man could tolerate. Dostoyevsky shrewdly observes in *The House of the Dead* "that if one wanted to crush, to annihilate a man utterly, to inflict on him the most terrible of punishments so that the most ferocious murderer would shudder at it and dread it beforehand, one need only give him work of an absolutely, completely useless and irrational character." If a man were condemned to pour water from one bucket to another and then back again, day after day, year after year, it would indeed drive him to despair. A life made up of actions that were devoid of all rational point or intent would be a maddening, meaningless life. But when traditional Christian philosophers talk about purpose and the purpose of life, they are not talking about having a purpose in that sense. They argue, as Cardinal Mercier and Professor Hick have argued, that man is a creature of God, created by God to worship Him, and to enter into a covenant with Him. That is man's purpose. It is in this sense that life must have a purpose if man is to achieve final happiness. Yet this sort of purpose is far more esoteric and metaphysical than the purpose Dostoyevsky was talking about. Religious moralists assume, as we have seen, that man has an essence or a *telos*—a purpose that he will realize if and only if he becomes what he was cut out by his Creator to become. It is not enough that we avoid the sort of situations Dostoyevsky alludes to, but we must fulfill our essence as well, for without this we will remain alienated and estranged.

But, as we have seen, this makes the groundless and perhaps even senseless assumption that man has a *telos* or an essence and that he will be happy when, and only when, he achieves it. Furthermore, the claim that man's life will lack purpose without God trades on a crucial ambiguity about 'purpose'. When it is claimed that without God life would have no purpose, the religious apologist is talking about a purpose for man *qua* man. He is trying to talk about man *qua* man having a purpose in the sense that an artifact, plumber, merchant, doctor, or policeman has a purpose. But it is far from clear that man has a purpose in that sense. It is also entirely unclear that

God = perfect good
must be good
is destruction — evil?

normative

↓

What
ought
to be
done
in all
case

descripti

↓

what
society
does
is it's
setup
practre

man must remain estranged, sensing to the full that his lot in the world is absurd, if he does not have such a purpose.

Many people feel that if man were not made for a purpose, his life must be without purpose. But here a spiritual malaise is being engendered by a conceptual confusion. Sometimes 'purpose' is used to mean function or role; but sometimes 'purpose' is used to indicate that an action was deliberately or intentionally done, that it was the carrying out of someone's aim or wish.

The second use of 'purpose'—the use that Dostoyevsky was talking about in our initial example—is such that we would say that only people and perhaps some animals could have it. When we use 'purpose' in this sense, we are speaking of people's goals, aims, intentions, motives and the like. 'Purpose' has this sense when we speak of our purpose in doing something specific: "What was your purpose in bringing home that dog?" and "I wonder what his purpose was in coming here?" Now this is one major way in which 'purpose' is used in which the theist and nontheist alike are in complete accord that there is a purpose in our lives—God or no God. And it is true that a life devoid of purpose in that sense would, without doubt, be a dreadful, senseless affair.

By contrast, we use 'purpose' in the first sense when we ask: "What is the purpose of that gadget in the kitchen?" or "What is the purpose of that fence along the road?" Here we imply "that someone did something, in the doing of which he had some purpose; namely, to bring about the thing with the purpose. Of course, *his* purpose is not identical with *its* purpose."[12] If we accept a scientific world picture and reject a theistic world picture, we are indeed forced to say that in this first sense life is purposeless. But it is completely contrary to the truth to say that a rejection of the theistic world view robs our lives of purpose in the second sense of 'purpose'. On the contrary, one could well claim, as Baier does, that "science has not only not robbed us of any purpose which we had before, but it has also furnished us with enormously greater power to achieve these purposes. Instead of praying for rain or a good harvest or offspring, we now use ice pellets, artificial manure, or artificial insemination."[13]

More importantly still, when we say "life must have a

purpose or there is no point in going on," we are usually using 'purpose' in the second sense. It is in this sense that we so desperately want life to have a purpose. But life can have a purpose in that sense in the twilight, or even in the complete absence, of the Gods. And whether or not something has or does not have a purpose in the first sense of 'purpose' does not matter at all, for having or lacking a purpose in this first sense carries neither *kudos* nor stigma. To say that a man has a purpose in this first sense is actually offensive for it involves treating man as a kind of tool or artifact. It is degrading for a man to be regarded as merely serving a purpose. If I turned to you and asked, "What are you for?" it would be insulting to you. It would be as if I had reduced you to "the level of a gadget, a domestic animal, or perhaps a slave."[14] I would be treating you merely as a means and not as an end. Failing to have a purpose in that sense does not at all detract from the meaningfulness of life. Many of us, at any rate, would be very disturbed and think our lives meaningless if we *did* have a purpose in this first sense.

The whole tendency to think that if there is no God and if God did not create man with a built-in design then life would be totally without worth arises from muddled thinking. People who claim that if God is dead nothing matters "mistakenly conclude that there can be no purpose *in* life because there is no purpose *of* life; that men cannot themselves adopt and achieve purposes because man, unlike a robot or a watchdog, is not a creature with a purpose."[15]

VI

There is a clash between the secular moralist and the Christian moralist over what will provide lasting contentment. While this may not always cause conflict over our usual daily activities, it is the source of a deeper moral conflict over what is worth seeking and how human life should be ordered. The Christian looks on life as something in which his ultimate goal or purpose as well as his basic purposes are set by God. We are, of course, free to reject this purpose, but unfailing happiness "is only to be found in participating in that consummation, in becoming the sort of person who is able to enter into final union with God."[16]

The intellectually harassed, non-Neanderthal, modern Christian is sorely tempted to give these strange claims a radical reinterpretation such that in some subtle sense religion becomes what it was for Matthew Arnold, "morality tinged with emotion." Religion on such a reinterpretation is envisaged as "morality strengthened and reinforced by the imagination and will."[17] For Braithwaite, a distinguished recent exponent of this view, to speak of "entering into final union with God"[18] amounts to an expression of intention to regard one's fellowmen in a brotherly way or to act as if all men were seeking to live together in peace and harmony. Religious utterances are generally not regarded as mysterious assertions about the nature of the universe, but as expressions of intention that we associate with certain parables. We may or may not believe the parables but we must at least be willing to allow the association. Such a reinterpretation may—as Jung would say—"breathe life into these ancient symbols," giving them new vitality for modern man questing for God. But such a coating to make religion respectable eats at the very substance of religion. If we finally go the way of Braithwaite, we have nothing left at all. MacIntyre rightly remarks, "such a view in reality renounces traditional religion altogether. For it omits from religion all reference to the reality of God, to God's real creating and redemptive acts. It preserves the name of religion while believing exactly what atheists believe."[19] If a Christian takes such a Braithwaitian turn, he will no longer have any ground at all for speaking of different expectations about life's goals; there will no longer be a ground in accordance with which a Christian moralist could set himself off from a secular moralist.

MacIntyre recognizes that both the reasonably orthodox Christian and the secularist are making claims about being, or a being, that in certain crucial respects are radically different and incompatible. The Christian, for example, trusts that there is a God who created him and who acts in the world while being 'out of' or 'beyond the world'. (Phrases like these are unintelligible to many secularists; the believer, to the contrary, will not allow that they are unintelligible, but often does assert with a certain Kierkegaardian joy and verve that they are extremely paradoxical. But, after all, what is faith without paradox?) Because of this 'fact' the Christian decides to act, to direct his life in a certain way. If he knows what he is about, he will recognize that what he is seeking is an alternative to another genuine morality that is quite independent of religion.

That there are these conflicting alternative moralities is very understandable, given the nature of religion. As we finally must just opt for belief or unbelief, so finally we must just decide whether to assent to a Christian way of life rather than to a secular one. There is no morally neutral vantage point from which we can judge and choose between these conflicting ways of life. When a Christian says that his morality is more adequate than a non-Christian's, he must rely on Christian standards of judgment. But MacIntyre would have us believe that the secular moralist is no better off here. He has no neutral haven that he can retreat to that will allow him to avoid the storm and stress of personal decision. For neither the Christian moralist nor the secularist is there a genuine safe port that will protect him from such blasts. There is no avoiding a decision when questions of conduct are at stake and there is no neutral ground from which we can decide what basic decisions we are to make. There is no morally neutral ground in accordance with which we can decide between sacred and secular principles of moral evaluation.

VII

Hick and MacIntyre have correctly indicated that, taken in its living context, Christianity (as all the historical religions) necessarily involves a way of life and a morality. The moral view inherent in Christianity sharply conflicts with secular morality (naturalism, atheism, humanism). If this moral view is deleted, the very heart of Christianity is destroyed. In that sense Christian morality is obviously not independent of the Christian religion. But even here we have an inversion of things. It is Christianity as a whole that could not exist without its distinctive morality. The moral aspect, or at least some of it, might be capable of survival without the rest of the religion. Presumably MacIntyre would say to this that Christian morality would be uprooted and lack an intelligible rationale if denied a distinctively Christian, or at least theistic, conception of the nature of things. And surely there is a very considerable warrant for such a claim. Christianity, of necessity, must have a definite moral point of view and Christian morality without Christian conceptions of man, history, and the cosmos is an absurdity that no rational man, "knight of faith" or not, ought to embrace. In this sense, Christian morality is not independent of Christianity as a whole.

This statement, however, is not in conflict with those claims for independence I developed in chapter 2. What has happened here is that there has been a confusion between two senses in which we can say morality is independent of religion. The first is the one mentioned in the last paragraph and in that sense it is false to say that all morality is independent of religion. To be a Christian is to accept a certain morality and to accept this morality involves accepting the central tenets of the Christian religion. To be a Christian in Christendom is to have certain distinctive general aims and a belief that man is a creature in God's care, created by God, with a God-given purpose. (Even here it remains the case that the Christian's varied moral claims do not follow from religious cosmological claims alone. Statements such as 'Love God with your whole heart and whole mind', 'The life of the spirit is good', 'Do not eat meat on Fridays', do not entail and are not entailed by statements like 'There must be a necessary being' or 'A transcendant being created the universe' or 'A being who created everything but Himself loves us'. Such Christian moral claims are footless, irrational moral claims without Christian belief.)

In a second and more fundamental sense, however, morality cannot be based on religion. This is the sense I discussed in chapter 2 and it is the sense most philosophers have had in mind when they have asserted the autonomy of morality from religion. The sense in which any morality is and must be independent of religion is this: that from the recognition and consequent statement that there is a being that some call 'God' no moral statements whatsoever follow. More generally, no moral statements at all can be derived from religious claims about what there is. This claim is not in conflict with the first sense in which it is correct to argue, as MacIntyre has, that morality is not independent of religion. (It is important, however, to note that this first sense could never serve as our basic meaning of what it is for something to be good, just, perfect or fair. In saying "Jesus is morally perfect" we are not saying "Jesus is Jesus." In saying "An uncreated Creator of the universe is good," we are not saying "An uncreated Creator of the universe is an uncreated Creator of the universe." Only if we independently understood what 'perfect' and 'good' meant could we make such claims. Our knowledge of good and evil cannot be derived from our knowledge of such a being.)

When we use the more familiar word 'God', a further complication arises. 'God' is characteristically used by believers with an evaluative force. 'God is worthy of worship', as we have seen, is characteristically used analytically, for in the contexts of Judeo-Christian religious assent and worship we would not say of any being, "my Lord and my God . . ." or "God I will follow Thee" or "God loves us and protects us" unless we believed that being to be worthy of worship. In most religious contexts, the use of the word 'God' connotes a being worthy of worship, but in deciding that there exists a being who is worthy of worship we must of necessity use our own moral insight. Knowledge that there is such a being is not, of course, just a matter of moral insight, but it essentially involves the making of a moral judgment. MacIntyre, in fine, has confused these two senses in which we can claim that morality is or is not independent of religion. In correctly seeing that in the first sense there is not this independence, MacIntyre thought that he had shown, in the second and more fundamental sense that I have distinguished, that there is no such independence. But in this last sense, it is incorrect to say that morality is dependent on religious beliefs; even Christian moral beliefs cannot be derived from them.

It is evident from MacIntyre's first paragraph that it is this second sense of independence that interests him. The intellectual issue he is interested in is precisely the one involved in this second sense in which we speak of the independence of morality from religion. MacIntyre points out that "Christianity consists of a number of assertions about what God is and what He has done and a number of injunctions about how we ought to live. In the New Testament, the latter are made to depend on the former."[20] MacIntyre wishes to establish this New Testament claim against the philosophic contention that the latter cannot be derived from the former and in that sense they do not depend on but are necessarily independent of the former. But, as we have shown, from definitional statements about God and from factual assertions about what God has done, is doing or will do, there follow no injunctions about how to live. And if we allow, as one crucial moral judgment, something like 'God is a Good Shepherd who watches over His flock', this judgment cannot in turn be derived from statements definitive of Godhood or factual assertions about what God does.

In sum, I have argued in this chapter that morality and religion are, in the crucial sense specified, logically independent—that is, we cannot derive moral claims from such cosmological claims as 'God exists', 'God shall raise the quick and the dead', and 'God laid the foundations of the earth'. 'X ought to be done' or 'X is good' is never identical with or derivable from 'God wills X' or 'God created X'. It is not senseless (conceptually unintelligible) to question the will of God, though it is blasphemous. I then went on to argue, as against Professor Hick, MacIntyre, and others, that a God-centered ethic has no claim to provide the most adequate criterion of moral actions because it possesses the deepest and most accurate understanding of man's condition. I argued that the claims to intelligibility and claims to truth given us by Christianity and Judaism are so scandalously weak that we have no grounds for using these religions as a basis for morality or as an answer to the "riddle of human destiny." Finally, I argued that there are no grounds for claiming that a man's life is without purpose if there is no God. In the only sense in which it really matters, we can and do have purposes in a Godless world.

NOTES

1. P. H. Nowell-Smith, "Morality: Religious and Secular" in *Rationalist Annual* (1961): 9.
2. To show this is one of the fundamental aims of Pascal's *Pensées*.
3. John Hick, "Belief and Life: The Fundamental Nature of the Christian Ethic," *Encounter* 20, no. 4 (1959): 494-516.
4. Alasdair MacIntyre, *Difficulties in Christian Belief* (London: SCM

Press, 1959), p. 107. It should be noted that MacIntyre has abandoned the position adumbrated in *Difficulties in Christian Belief* and has come to adopt a view very similar to my own. See his contribution in Alasdair MacIntyre and Paul Ricoeur, *The Religious Significance of Atheism* (New York and London: Columbia University Press, 1969.)

5. Hick (1959), op. cit., p. 495.

6. Ibid., pp. 498-99.

7. Exactly the same considerations hold for mystical experiences.

8. See his forceful inaugural lecture, "Theology's Central Problem," Birmingham, 1967.

9. On this point, see Kai Nielsen, "Can Faith Validate God-Talk?" in *Theology Today*, 20, no. 2 (July 1963): 158-73.

10. Ronald Hepburn has some very effective things to say against this argument. See Ronald Hepburn, *Christianity and Paradox* (London: C. A. Watts, 1958), pp. 147-54.

11. See Kurt Baier, "The Meaning of Life," inaugural lecture, Canberra, 1957.

12. Ibid., p. 19.

13. Ibid., p. 20.

14. Ibid.

15. Ibid.

16. MacIntyre (1959), op. cit., p. 107.

17. Ibid., p. 104.

18. R. B. Braithwaite, *An Empiricist's View of the Nature of Religious Belief* (London: Cambridge University Press, 1955).

19. MacIntyre (1959), op. cit., p. 105.

20. Ibid., p. 104.

5

Humanistic Ethics

I

There are fundamental difficulties and perhaps even elements of incoherence in Christian ethics, but what can a secular moralist offer in its stead? Religious morality—and Christian morality in particular—may have its difficulties, but religious apologists argue that secular morality has still greater difficulties. It leads, they claim, to ethical skepticism, nihilism, or, at best, to a pure conventionalism. Such apologists could point out that if we look at morality with the cold eye of an anthropologist, we will find morality to be nothing more than the often conflicting *mores* of the various tribes spread around the globe.

If we eschew the kind of insight that religion can give us, we will have no Archimedean point in accordance with which we can decide how it is that we ought to live and die. If we look at ethics from such a purely secular point of view, we will discover that it is constituted by tribal conventions, conventions that we are free to reject if we are sufficiently free from ethnocentrism. We can continue to act in accordance with them or we can reject them and adopt a different set of conventions; but whether we act in accordance with the old conventions or forge "new tablets," we are still acting in accordance with certain conventions. In relation to these conventions certain acts are right or wrong, reasonable or unreasonable, but we cannot justi-

113

fy the fundamental moral conventions themselves or the ways of life which they partially codify.

When these points are conceded, theologians are in a position to press home a powerful apologetic point: when we become keenly aware of the true nature of such conventionalism and when we become aware that there is no overarching purpose that men were destined to fulfill, the myriad purposes, the aims and goals humans create for themselves, will be seen to be inadequate. When we realize that life does not have a meaning that is there to be found, but that we human beings must by our deliberate decisions give it whatever meaning it has, we will (as Sartre so well understood) undergo estrangement and despair. We will drain our cup to its last bitter drop and feel our alienation to the full. Perhaps there are human purposes, purposes to be found in life, and we can and do have them even in a Godless world; but without God there can be no one overarching purpose, no one basic scheme of human existence in virtue of which we could find a meaning for our grubby lives. It is this overall sense of meaning that man so ardently strives for, but it is not to be found in a purely secular worldview. You secularists, a new Pascal might argue, must realize, if you really want to be clear-headed, that no purely human purposes are ultimately worth striving for. What you humanists can give us by way of a scheme of human existence will always be a poor second-best and not what the human heart most ardently longs for.

The considerations for and against an ethics not rooted in a religion are complex and involuted; a fruitful discussion of them is difficult, for in considering the matter of our passions, our anxieties, our ultimate concerns (if you will) are involved, and they tend to blur our vision, enfeeble our understanding of what exactly is at stake. But we must not forget that what is at stake here is just what kind of ultimate commitments or obligations a man could have without evading any issue, without self-deception or without delusion. I shall be concerned to display and assess, to make plain and also to weigh, some of the most crucial considerations for and against a purely secular ethic. While I shall try to make clear in an objective fashion what the central issues are, I shall also give voice to my reflective convictions on this matter. I shall try to make evident my reasons for believing that we do not need God or any religious belief to support our moral convictions. I shall do this, as I think one should in philosophy, by making apparent the dialectic of the problem, the considerations for and against, and by arguing for what I take to be their proper resolution.

II

I am aware that crisis theologians would claim that I am being naive, but I do not see why purposes of purely human devising are not ultimately worth striving for. There is much that we humans prize and would continue to prize even in a Godless world. Many things would remain to give our lives meaning and point even after "the death of God."

Take a simple example. All of us want to be happy. But in certain bitter or skeptical moods we question what happiness is or we despairingly ask ourselves whether anyone can really be happy. Is this, however, a sober, sane view of the situation? I do not think that it is. Indeed, we cannot adequately define 'happiness' in the way that we can 'bachelor', but neither can we in that way define 'chair', 'wind', 'pain', and the vast majority of words in everyday discourse. For words like 'bachelor', 'triangle', or 'father' we can specify a consistent set of properties that all the things and only the things denoted by these words have, but we cannot do this for 'happiness', 'chair', 'pain', and the like. Yet there is no great loss here. Modern philosophical analysis has taught us that such an essentially Platonic conception of definition is unrealistic and unnecessary.[1] I may not be able to define 'chair' in the way that I can define 'bachelor', but I understand the meaning of chair perfectly well. In normal circumstances, at least, I know what to sit on when someone tells me to take a chair. I may not be able to define 'pain', but I know what it is like to be in pain and sometimes I can know when others are in pain. Similarly, though I cannot define 'happiness' in the same way that I can define 'bachelor', I know what it is like to be happy, and sometimes I can judge with considerable reliability whether others are happy or sad. 'Happiness' is a slippery word, but it is not so slippery that we are justified in saying that nobody knows what happiness is.

A man could be said to have lived a happy life if he had found lasting sources of satisfaction in his life and if he had been able to find certain goals worthwhile and to achieve at least some of them. He could indeed have suffered some pain and anxiety, but his life, for the most part, must have been free from pain, estrangement and despair and must, on balance, have been a life that he has liked and found worthwhile. Surely we have no good grounds for saying that no one achieves such a balance or that no one is ever happy even for a time. We all have some idea of what would make us happy and of what would make us unhappy; many people, at least, can remain happy even after "the death of God." At any rate, we need not strike Pascalian attitudes, for even in a purely secular world there are permanent sources of human happiness of which anyone may avail himself.

What are these relatively permanent sources of human happiness that we all want or need? What is it that, if we have it, will give us the basis for a life that could properly be said to be happy? We all desire to be free from pain and want. [Even masochists do not seek pain for its own sake; they endure pain because this is the only psychologically acceptable way of achieving something else (usually sexual satisfaction) that is so gratifying to them that they will put up with the pain to achieve it.] We all want a life in which sometimes we can enjoy ourselves and in which we can attain our fair share of some of the simple pleasures that we all desire. They are not everything in life, but they are important, and our lives would be impoverished without them.

We also need security and emotional peace. We need and want a life in which we will not be constantly threatened with physical or emotional harassment. Again, this is not the only thing worth seeking, but it is an essential ingredient in any adequate picture of the good life.

Human love and companionship are also central to a happy life. We prize them and a life without them is most surely an impoverished life, a life that no man, if he would take the matter to heart, would desire. But I would most emphatically assert that human love and companionship are quite possible in a Godless world, and the fact that life will some day inexorably come to an end and cut off love and companionship altogether enhances rather than diminishes their present value.

Furthermore, we all need some sort of creative employment or meaningful work to give our lives point, to save them from boredom, drudgery and futility. A man who can find no way to use the talents he has, or a man who can find no work that is meaningful to him, will indeed be a miserable man. But again there is work—whether it be as a surgeon, a farmer, or a fisherman—that has a rationale even in a world without God. And poetry, music, and art retain their beauty and enrich our lives even in the complete absence of God or the gods.

We want and need art, music, and the dance. We find pleasure in travel and conversation and in a rich variety of experiences. The sources of human enjoyment are obviously too numerous to detail, but all of them are achievable in a God-less universe. If some can be ours, we can attain a reasonable measure of happiness. Only a Steppenwolfish personality, beguiled by impossible expectations and warped by irrational guilts and fears, can fail to find happiness in the realization of such ends. But to be free of impossible expectations people must clearly recognize that there is no "one big thing" (or, for that matter, "one small thing") that would make them permanently happy; almost anything permanently and exclusively pursued will lead to that nausea that Sartre has so forcefully brought to our attention. But we can, if we are not too sick and if our situation is not too precarious, find lasting sources of human happiness in a purely secular world.

It is not only happiness for ourselves that can give us something of value, but there is the need to do what we can to diminish the awful sum of human misery in the world. I have never understood those who say that they find contemporary life meaningless because they find nothing worthy to which they can devote their energies. Throughout the world there is an immense amount of human suffering, suffering that can be partially alleviated through a variety of human efforts. Why can we not find a meaningful life in devoting ourselves, as did Doctor Rieux in Albert Camus's *La Peste,* to relieving somewhat the sum total of human suffering? Why cannot this give our lives point and an overall rationale? It is childish to think that by human effort we will some day totally rid the world of suffering and hate, of deprivation and sadness; they are a permanent feature of the human condition. But specific instances of human suffering can be alleviated. The plague is always potentially with us, but we can destroy the Nazis and we can fight for racial and social equality throughout the world. And as isolated people, as individuals in a mass society, we find people turning to us in dire need, in suffering and in emotional deprivation, and we can as individuals respond to those people and alleviate or at least acknowledge that suffering and deprivation. A man who says, "If God is dead, nothing matters," is a spoilt child who has never looked at his fellowman with compassion.

Yet, it might be objected, if we abandon a Judeo-Christian *Weltanschauung,* there can, in a secular world, be no "one big thing" to give our lives an overall rationale. We will not be able to see written in the stars the final significance of human effort. There will be no architectonic purpose to give our lives such a rationale. Like Tolstoy's Pierre in *War and Peace,* we desire somehow to gather the sorry scheme of things entire into one intelligible explanation so that we can finally crack the riddle of human destiny. We long to understand why it is that men suffer and die. If it is a factual answer that is wanted when such a question is asked, the answer is evident enough: ask any physician. But clearly that is no answer to people who seek such a general account of human existence. They want some justification for suffering; they want some way of showing that suffering is after all for a good purpose. It can, of course, be argued that suffering sometimes is a good thing, for it occasionally gives us insight and at times even brings about in the man who suffers an increased capacity to love and to be kind. But there is plainly an excessive amount of human suffering— the suffering of children in hospitals, the suffering of people devoured by cancer and the sufferings of millions of Jews under the Nazis—for which there simply is no justification. Neither the religious man nor the secularist can explain, that is, justify, such suffering and find some overall scheme of life in which it has some place, but only the religious man needs to do so. The secularist understands that suffering is not something to be justified but simply to be struggled against with courage and dignity. And in this fight, even the man who has been deprived of that which could give him some measure of happiness can still find or make for himself a meaningful human existence.

III

I have argued that purely human purposes—those goals we set for ourselves, the intentions we form—are enough to give meaning to our lives.[2] We desire happiness and we can find, even in a purely secular world, abundant sources of it. Beyond this we can find a rationale for seeking to mitigate the awful burden of human suffering. These two considerations are enough to make life meaningful. But it might be objected that I have put far too great a stress on the value of human happiness; that there are other considerations in life, other values that are intrinsically worthwhile. We desire self-consciousness and some sense of self-identity as well as happiness. And we do not desire them for the enjoyment and happiness that will come from them but for their own sakes.

I am inclined to agree that this is so; human happiness and the desire to avoid suffering are central but are not the only facets of morality. To acknowledge this, however, only complicates the secular picture of morality: it gives us no reason to bring in theistic concepts. I admire human beings who are non-evasive and who have a sense of their own identity, and I regard an understanding of myself as something to be prized for its own sake. I do not need a deity to support this appreciation or give it value.

Philosophers, and some theologians as well, might challenge what I have said in a slightly different way. It could be said that even if we add consciousness as another intrinsic good, there is not the close connection between happiness and self-awareness on the one hand and virtue or moral good on the other that I have claimed there is. That men do seek happiness as an end is one thing; that they ought to seek it as an end is another. As G. E. Moore has in effect shown,[3] we cannot derive 'X is good' from 'People desire X' or from 'X makes people happy', for it is always meaningful to ask whether or not happiness is good and whether or not we ought to seek it for its own sake. It will be argued that I, like all secularists, have confused factual and moral issues. An 'ought' cannot be derived from an 'is'; we cannot deduce that something is good from a discovery that it will make people happy. My hypothetical critic could well go on to claim that we must first justify the fundamental claim that happiness is good. Do we really have any reason to believe that happiness is good? Is the secularist in any more of a position to justify his claim than is the religionist to justify his claim that whatever God wills is good?

I would first like to point out that I have not confused factual and moral issues. One of the basic reasons I have for rejecting either a natural-law ethics or an ethics of divine commands is that both systematically confuse factual and moral issues. We cannot deduce that people ought to do something from discovering that they do it or seek it; nor can we conclude from the proposition that a being exists whom people call God that we ought to do whatever that being commands. In both cases we unjustifiably pass from a factual premise to a moral conclusion. Moral statements are not factual statements about what people seek or avoid, or about what a deity commands. But we do justify moral claims by an appeal to factual claims, and there is a close connection between what human beings desire on reflection and what they deem to be good. 'X is good' does not mean 'X makes for happiness', but in deciding that something is good, it is crucial to know what makes human beings happy. Both the Christian moralist and the secular moralist lay stress on human happiness. The Christian moralist—St. Augustine and Pascal are perfect examples—argues that only the Christian has a clear insight into what human happiness really is and that there is no genuine happiness without God. But, as I argued in chapter 4, we have no valid grounds for believing that only in God can we find happiness and that there are no stable sources of human happiness apart from God.

I cannot prove that happiness is good, but Christian and non-Christian alike take it in practice to be a very fundamental good. I can only appeal to your sense of psychological realism to persuade you to admit intellectually what in practice you acknowledge, namely, that happiness is good and that pointless suffering is bad. If you will acknowledge this, you must accept that I have shown that man can attain happiness even in a world without God.

Suppose some Dostoyevskian "underground man" does not care a fig about happiness. Suppose he does not even care about the sufferings of others. How, then, can you show him to be wrong? But suppose a man does not care about God or about doing what He commands either. How can you show that such an indifference to God is wrong? If we ask such abstract questions, we can see a crucial feature about the nature of morality. Sometimes a moral agent may reach a point at which he can give no further justification for his claims but must simply, by his own deliberate decision, resolve to take a certain position. Here the claims of the existentialists have a genuine relevance. We come to recognize that, in the last analysis, nothing can take the place of a decision or resolution. In the end, we must simply decide. This recognition may arouse our anxieties and stimulate rationalization, but the necessity of making a decision is inherent in the logic of the situation. Actually, the religious moralist is in a worse position than the secularist, for he not only needs to subscribe to the principle that human happiness is good and that pain and suffering have no intrinsic value; he must also subscribe to the *outré* claims that only in God can man find happiness and that one ought to do whatever it is that God commands. 'Man can find lasting happiness only if he turns humbly to his Savior' has the look of a factual statement and is a statement that most assuredly calls for some kind of rational support. It is not something we must or can simply decide about. But the assertion that one ought to do what is commanded by God, like the assertion that happiness is good, does appear simply to call for a decision for or against. But what it is that one is deciding for when one "decides for God or for Christ" is so obscure as to be scarcely intelligible. Furthermore, the man who subscribes to that religious principle must subscribe to the secular claim as well. But why subscribe to this obscure second principle when there is no evidence at all for the claim that man can find happiness only in God?

Morality is not science. Moral claims direct our actions; they tell us how we ought to act; they do not simply describe what we seek or explain our preferential behavior.[4] A secular morality need not view morality as a science or as an activity that is simply descriptive or explanatory. It can and should remain a normative activity. Secular morality starts with the assumption that happiness and self-awareness are fundamental human goods and that pain and suffering are never desirable in themselves. It may finally be impossible to prove that this is so, but if people will be honest with themselves they will see that in their behavior they clearly show that they subscribe to such a principle; and a philosopher can demonstrate that criticisms of such moral principles rest on confusions. Finally, I have tried to show that a man with secular knowledge alone can find clear and permanent sources of happiness such that whoever will avail himself of these sources of happiness can, if he is fortunate, lead a happy and purposeful life.

IV

The dialectic of our problem has not ended. The religious moralist might acknowledge that human happiness is indeed plainly a good thing while contending that secular morality, where it is consistent and reflective, will inevitably lead to some variety of egoism. An individual who recognized the value of happiness and self-consciousness might, if he were free of religious restraints, ask himself why he should be concerned with the happiness and self-awareness of others, except where their happiness and self-awareness would contribute to his own good. We must face the fact that sometimes, as the world goes, people's interests clash. Sometimes the common good is served only at the expense of some individual's interests. An individual must therefore, in such a circumstance, sacrifice what will make him happy for the common good. Morality requires this sacrifice of us, when it is necessary for the common good; morality, any morality, exists in part at least to adjudicate between the conflicting interests and demands of people. It is plainly evident that everyone cannot be happy all the time and that sometimes one person's happiness or the happiness of a group is at the expense of another person's happiness.

Morality requires that we attempt to distribute happiness as evenly as possible. We must be fair: each person is to count for one and none is to count for more than one. Whether we like a person or not, whether he is useful to his society or not, his interests and what will make him happy, must be considered in any final decision as to what ought to be done. The requirements of justice make it necessary that each person be given equal consideration. I cannot justify my neglect of another person in some matter of morality simply on the grounds that I do not like him, that he is not a member of my set or that he is not a productive member of society. The religious apologist will argue that behind these requirements of justice as fairness there lurks the ancient religious principle that men are creatures of God, each with an infinite worth, and that men are never to be treated only as means but as persons deserving of respect in their own right. They have an infinite worth simply as persons.

My religious critic, following out the dialectic of the problem, should query why you should respect someone, why you should treat all people equally, if doing this is not in your interest or not in the interests of your group. No purely secular justification can be given for so behaving. My critic now serves his *coup de grâce:* the secularist, as does the "knight of faith," acknowledges that the principle of respect for persons is a precious one—a principle that he is unequivocally committed to, but the religious man alone can justify adherence to this principle. The secularist is surreptitiously drawing on Christian inspiration when he insists that all men should be considered equal and that people's rights must be respected. For a secular morality to say all it wants and needs to say, it must, at this crucial point, be parasitical upon a God-centered morality. Without such a dependence on religion, secular morality collapses into egoism.

It may well be the case that, as a historical fact, our moral concern for persons came from our religious conceptions, but it is a well-known principle of logic that the validity of a belief is independent of its origin. What the religious moralist must do is to show that only on religious grounds could such a principle of respect for persons be justifiably asserted. But he has not shown that this is so; and there are good reasons for thinking that it is not so. Even if the secularist must simply subscribe to the Kantian principle, 'Treat every man as an end and never as a means only', as he must subscribe to the claim, 'Happiness is good', it does not follow that he is on worse ground than the religious moralist, for the religious moralist, too, as we have seen, must simply subscribe to his ultimate moral principle, 'Always do what God wills'.

In a way, the religious moralist's position here is simpler than the secularist's, for he needs only the fundamental moral principle that he ought to do what God wills. The secularist appears to need at least two fundamental principles. But in another and more important way the religious moralist's position is more complex, for he must subscribe to the extraordinarily obscure notion that man is a creature of God and as such has infinite worth. The Kantian principle may in the last analysis simply require subscription, but it is not inherently mysterious. To accept it does not require a crucifixion of the intellect. And if we are prepared simply to commit ourselves to one principle, why not to two principles, neither of which involves any appeal to conceptions whose very intelligibility is seriously in question?

The above argument is enough to destroy the believer's case here. But need we even rely on a historically religious concern as the basis for our moral position? There is a purely secular rationale for treating people fairly, for regarding them as persons. Let me show how this is so. We have no evidence that men ever lived in a pre-social state of nature. Man, as we know him, is an animal with a culture, he is part of a community, and the very concept of community implies binding principles and regulations—duties, obligations and rights. Yet, imaginatively we could conceive, in broad outline at any rate, what it would be like to live in a pre-social state.

In such a state no one would have any laws or principles to direct his behavior. In that sense, man would be completely free. But such a life, as Hobbes graphically depicted, would be a clash of rival egoisms. Life in that state of nature would be, in his celebrated phrase, "nasty, brutish, and short." Now if men were in such a state and if they were perfectly rational egoists, what kind of community life would they choose, given the fact that they were, very roughly speaking, nearly equal in strength and ability? (The fact that in communities as we find them men are not so nearly equal in power is beside the point for our hypothetical situation.) Given that they all start from scratch and have roughly equal abilities, it seems to me that it would be most reasonable, even for rational egoists, to band together into a community where each man's interests were given equal consideration, where each person was treated as deserving of respect.[5]

Each rational egoist would want others to treat him with respect, for his very happiness is contingent upon that; and he would recognize that he could attain the fullest cooperation of others only if other rational egoists knew or had good grounds for believing that their interests and their persons would also be respected. Such cooperation is essential for each egoist if all are to have the type of community life that would give them the best chance of satisfying their own interests to the fullest degree. Thus, even if men were thorough egoists, we would still have rational grounds for subscribing to a principle of respect for persons. That men are not thoroughly rational, do not live in a state of nature, and are not thorough egoists does not gainsay the fact that we have rational grounds for regarding social life, organized in accordance with such a principle, as being objectively better than a social life which ignores this principle. The point here is that even rational egoists could see that this is the best possible social organization where men are nearly equal in ability.

What about the world we live in—a world in which, given certain extant social relationships, men are not equal or even nearly equal in power and opportunity? What reason is there for an egoist who is powerfully placed to respect the rights of others, when they cannot hurt him? We can say that his position, no matter how strong, might change and he might then need his rights protected; but this is surely not a strong enough reason for respecting human rights. To be moral involves respecting those rights, but our rational egoist may not propose to be moral. In considering such questions, we reach a point in reasoning at which we must simply decide what sort of person we shall strive to become. The religious moralist also reaches the same point. He, too, must make a decision of principle, but the principle he adopts is a fundamentally incoherent one. He not only must decide, but his decision must involve the acceptance of an absurdity.

It is sometimes argued by religious apologists that men will respect the rights of others only if they fear a wrathful and angry God. Without such a punitive sanction or threat, men will go wild. Yet it hardly seems to be the case that Christians, with their fear of hell, have been any better at respecting the rights of others than non-Christians. A study of the Middle Ages or the conquest of the non-Christian world makes this plain enough. And even if it were true that Christians were better in this respect than non-Christians, it would not show that they had a superior moral reason for their behavior, for in so acting and in so reasoning, they are not giving a morally relevant reason at all but are simply acting out of fear for their own hides. Yet Christian morality supposedly takes us beyond the clash of the rival egoisms of secular life.

In short, Christian ethics has not been able to give us a sounder ground for respecting persons than we have with a purely secular morality. The Kantian principle of respect for persons is actually bound up in the very idea of morality, either secular or religious; and there are good reasons, of a perfectly mundane sort, why we should have the institution of morality as we now have it, namely, that our individual welfare is dependent on having a device that equitably resolves social and individual conflicts. Morality has an objective rationale in complete independence of religion. Even if God is dead, it does not really matter.

It is in just this last thrust, it might be objected, that you reveal your true colors and show your own inability to face a patent social reality. At this point the heart of your rationalism is very irrational. For millions of people, "the death of God" means very much. It really does matter. In the secularist's somewhat technical sense, the concept of God may be chaotic or unintelligible, but this concept, embedded in our languages—embedded in "the stream of life"—has an enormous social significance for many people. Jews and Christians, if they take their religion to heart, could not but feel a great rift in their lives with the loss of God, for they have indeed organized their lives around their religion. Their very life-ideals have grown out of these concepts. What should have been said is that if "God is dead" it matters a lot, but nevertheless we should stand up like men and face this loss and learn to live in the post-Christian era. As Nietzsche so well knew, to do this involves a basic reorientation of one's life and not just an intellectual dissent from a few statements of doctrine.

There is truth in such an objection and a kind of 'empiricism about man' that philosophers are prone to neglect. Of course it matters when one recognizes that one's religion is illusory. For a devout Jew or Christian to give up his God most certainly is important and does take him into the abyss of a spiritual crisis. But in saying that God's death does not really matter, I was implying what I have argued for in this essay; namely, that if an erstwhile believer loses his God but can keep his nerve, think the matter over, and thoroughly take it to heart, life can still be meaningful and morality can yet have an objective rationale. Surely, for good psychological reasons, he is prone to doubt this argument, but if he will only "hold on to his brains" and keep his courage, he will come to see that it is so. In this crucial sense it remains true that if "God is dead" it does not really matter.

NOTES

1. This is convincingly argued in Michael Scriven's "Definitions, Explanations and Theories" in H. Feigl, M. Scriven, and G. Maxwell, *Minnesota Studies in the Philosophy of Science,* vol. 2. (Minneapolis: University of Minnesota Press, 1958), pp. 99-195.
2. I have argued this point in considerably more detail in Kai Nielsen, "Linguistic Philosophy and 'The Meaning of Life'," *Cross Currents* 15, no. 3 (1964): 313-34.
3. G. E. Moore, *Principia Ethica* (Cambridge: Cambridge University Press, 1903), chapters 1 and 2.
4. This crucial claim is ably argued by P. H. Nowell-Smith, *Ethics,* (London: Blackwell, 1957), chapters 1-4; by John Ladd, "Reason and Practice," in John Wild, (ed.), *The Return to Reason* (Chicago: Chicago University Press, 1953) pp. 253-358; and by A. E. Murphy, "The Common Good," in *Proceedings and Addresses of the American Philosophy Association* 24 (1950-1951): pp. 3-18.
5. Some of the very complicated considerations relevant here have been brought out subtly by John Rawls's "Justice as Fairness," in *The Philosophical Review* 57 (1958): pp. 164-94, and by Georg von Wright, *The Varieties of Goodness* (London: Routledge, 1963), chapter 10. I think it could be reasonably maintained that my argument is more vulnerable here than at any other point. I would not, of course, use it if I did not think it could be sustained; but if anyone should find unconvincing the argument as presented here, I would beg him to consider the argument that precedes it and the one that immediately follows it. They alone are sufficient to establish my general case.

6

The Search for Absolutes

In the previous chapter it was reasonably evident that my ethical theory relies on certain judgments about what is intrinsically good (about what is worth having or worth seeking for its own sake) in deciding what set of ultimate commitments are worthy of adoption or what set of aims a man should pursue. Happiness, self-consciousness, a sense of self-identity were the main candidates for intrinsic goodness. These things are taken to be intrinsically good because, when we are tolerably clear about the distinction between desiring something only as a means and desiring something as an end as well, they are what we would on reflection desire for their own sakes. Happiness, self-consciousness, a sense of self-identity are essential to give significance to human living; without them or the hope of their attainment, human life would not be worth living and bare human survival would be utterly pointless.

However, it is often thought that such a conception of the moral life has detestable implications which, when squarely faced, make it untenable. These implications apply to all such humanistic views, which in crucial respects are heir to the assumptions of utilitarianism. And while my view is not, strictly speaking, utilitarian, it is close enough to it to share these defects or alleged defects.

What are these alleged defects that are supposed to under-

128

mine my view and even so humane a system of morality as John Stuart Mill's? I am, in effect, giving you to understand that actions, rules, policies, practices and moral principles are ultimately to be judged by certain consequences: to wit, whether doing them more than, or at least as much as, doing anything else or acting in accordance with them more than, or at least as much as, acting in accordance with alternative principles, tends, on the whole, and for everyone involved, to maximize satisfaction, that is, to maximize happiness, minimize pain, enhance self-consciousness and preserve one's sense of self-identity. The states of affairs to be sought are those which maximize these things to the greatest extent possible for all mankind. But while this all sounds very humane and humanitarian, it has been forcefully argued that, when its implications are thought through, it will be seen actually to have inhumane and morally intolerable implications. On such a utilitarian or quasi-utilitarian view, circumstances *could* arise in which one would have to assert that one was justified in punishing, killing, torturing, or deliberately harming the innocent and such a consequence is, morally speaking, unacceptable.[1] As Anscombe (whose views I discussed in chapter 2) has put it, anyone who "really thinks, in advance, that it is open to question whether such an action as procuring the judicial execution of the innocent should be quite excluded from consideration—I do not want to argue with him; he shows a corrupt mind."[2] Presumably such a view as I have been arguing has horrendous consequences; when I and others committed to such utilitarian or quasi-utilitarian ethical theories become fully aware of such consequences, we will abandon, if we have any moral sensitivity, nay, any plain humanity at all, such wayward ethical theories.

At the risk of being thought to exhibit a corrupt mind and a shallow consequentialist morality, I should like to argue that things are not as simple and straightforward as Anscombe seems to believe.

Surely every moral man must be appalled at the judicial execution of the innocent or at the punishment, torture, and killing of the innocent. Indeed, being appalled by such behavior partially defines what it is to be a moral agent. And I, as well as the utilitarian, have very good utilitarian grounds for being so appalled, namely, that it is always wrong to inflict pain for its own sake. But this does not get to the core considerations which divide a Christian absolutism such as Anscombe's from a humanist and quasi-utilitarian account of morality such as my own. There is a series of tough cases that need to be taken to heart and their implications thought through by any reflective person interested in morality, with or without God. By such investigation we can get to the heart of the issue between such an absolutism and my kind of consequentialism. Consider the clash between moral absolutism and utilitarianism arising over the problem of a 'just war'.

> If we deliberately bomb civilian targets, we do not pretend that civilians are combatants in any simple fashion, but argue that this bombing will terminate hostilities more quickly, and will minimize all around suffering. It is hard to see how any brand of utilitarianism will escape Miss Anscombe's objections. We are certainly killing the innocent . . . we are not killing them for the sake of killing them, but to save the lives of other innocent persons. Utilitarians, I think, grit their teeth and put up with this as part of the logic of total war; Miss Anscombe and anyone who thinks like her surely has to either redescribe the situation to ascribe guilt to the civilians or else she has to refuse to accept this sort of military tactic as simply wrong.[3]

It is indeed true that we cannot but feel the force of Miss Anscombe's objections. But is it the case that anyone shows a corrupt mind if he defends such bombing when, horrible as it is, it will quite definitely lessen appreciably the total amount of suffering and death in the long run, and if he is sufficiently nonevasive not to rationalize such a bombing of civilians into a situation in which all the putatively innocent people—children and all—are somehow in some measure judged guilty? Must it be the case that he exhibits a corrupt moral sense if he refuses to hold that such military tactics are never morally justified? Must this be the monstrous view of a fanatical man devoid of any proper moral awareness? It is difficult for me to believe that this must be so.

Consider the quite parallel actions of guerrilla fighters and terrorists in wars of national liberation. In certain, almost unavoidable circumstances, they must deliberately kill the innocent. We need to see some cases in detail here to get the necessary contextual background and for this reason the motion picture *The Battle of Algiers* can be taken as a convenient point of reference. In that film Algerian women—gentle women with children of their own and plainly people of moral sensitivity—with evident heaviness of heart, planted bombs that they had every reason to believe would kill innocent people, including children; a French general, also a human being of moral fiber and integrity, ordered the torture of Arab terrorists or suspected terrorists and threatened the bombing of houses in which terrorists were concealed but which also contained innocent people, including children. There are indeed many people involved in such activities who are cruel, sadistic beasts or simply largely morally indifferent or, in important ways, morally uncomprehending. But the characters I referred to from *The Battle of Algiers* were not of that stamp. They were moral agents of a high degree of sensitivity and yet they deliberately killed or were prepared to kill the innocent. And, with insignificant variations, this is a recurrent phenomenon of human living in extreme situations. Such cases are by no means desert island or esoteric cases.

It is indeed arguable that such actions are always morally wrong—whether anyone should ever act as the Arab women or the French general acted. But what could not be reasonably maintained, *pace* Anscombe, by any stretch of the imagination is that the characters I described from *The Battle of Algiers* exhibited corrupt minds. Possibly morally mistaken, yes; guilty of moral corruption, no.

Dropping the charge of moral corruption, but sticking with the moral issue about what actions are right, is it not the case that my consequentialist position logically forces me to conclude that under some circumstances—where the good to be achieved is great enough—I must not only countenance but actually advocate such violence toward the innocent? But is it not always, no matter what the circumstances or consequences, wrong even to countenance such violence, let alone to speak of advocating it or engaging in it? To answer such a question affirmatively is to commit oneself to the kind of moral absolutism that Miss Anscombe advocates. Given the alternatives, should not one be such an absolutist or at least hold that certain deontological principles (principles of right and wrong) must never be overridden?

I will take the papal bull by the horns, so to speak, and answer that there are circumstances when such violence must be reluctantly assented to or even taken to be something that one, morally speaking, must do. This very much needs arguing and I shall argue it, but first I would like to set out some further cases that have a similar bearing. They are by contrast artificial cases. Some of them, for someone who has a macabre sense of humor, might even seem funny, but I use them not to cause offense or to engage in a form of sick humor; rather, with their greater simplicity, by contrast with my above examples, there are fewer variables to control and I can more readily make the essential conceptual and moral points. But I shall neither forget nor neglect our more complex case.

II

Consider the following rather varied cases embedded in their exemplary tales.

1. The Case of the Innocent Fat Man

Consider the story (well known to philosophers) of the fat man stuck in the mouth of a cave on a coast. He was leading a group of people out of the cave when he stuck in the mouth of the cave. In a very short time high tide will be upon them and unless he is promptly unstuck, they all will be drowned except the fat man, whose head is out of the cave. Fortunately or unfortunately, someone has with him a stick of dynamite. The short of the matter is, either they use the dynamite and blast the poor innocent fat man out of the mouth of the cave or everyone else drowns; either one life or many lives.

Our Christian absolutist presumably would take the attitude that it is all in God's hands and say that they ought never to blast the fat man out, for it is always wrong to kill the innocent. Must or should a moral man come to that conclusion? I shall argue that he should not.

2. The Case of the Dispensable Oldster

There are five shipwrecked people on a life raft. All are of sound health, with people who love and depend on them at home, except for one ill old man slowly dying of cancer and whose relatives and close friends are all dead. Suppose further that the sea is getting rough and that it is as evident as anything can be that (*a*) they will not soon be rescued and (*b*) unless one man gets out into the freezing waters, the raft will be swamped.

Suppose they deliberate about what to do. If they do and they do it honestly and if the situation is as I have hypothesized, it seems to me perfectly evident that if they are deliberating morally, they should all decide—innocent though he is—that the old man should be sacrificed (he should jump overboard); and that if he does not agree to this that he should be forced to go overboard.[4] In the first instance, an innocent man is allowed to die (we forbear to prevent his death) and in the second instance (where he is forced overboard) an innocent man is killed. In the last instance we have gone against the principle of some Christian absolutists that the direct intention of the death of an innocent person is never justifiable. The rationale for what from a Christian point of view is a thoroughly immoral action is that moral reflection on the balance of good over evil makes it evident that this course of action is required from the moral point of view. The suffering and death of the innocent man is evil enough, but the more extensive death and suffering resulting from his not killing himself or being killed is a still worse evil. Ask yourself, if you were that old man, what you would feel incumbent on yourself to do.

3. Der Übermensch on a Life Raft

There are two men in a life raft. One is simply a plain man (a plain banker, teacher, car dealer, trolley-car conductor), the other a scientist on the verge of making a major discovery in cancer research that will lead to a breakthrough in the treatment of the disease. Where it is impossible that they both can live in such a situation, a consequentialist ethic like my own is committed to saying that the scientist should protect his life even by killing the plain man, if it becomes necessary.

Many regard this attitude as morally offensive. All people, it is maintained, are of equal worth and have equal rights. We cannot simply sacrifice another man in such a manner. Morally speaking, we cannot simply sacrifice him in any manner. That people in life and in *The Last Exit to Brooklyn* are treated differently only proves what any tolerably realistic man should know: the moral ordering of things is frequently grossly disregarded. To think that we can justifiably sacrifice a man in this way is to abandon moral principle and, we are told, to play God. It is never right to sacrifice an innocent man to rescue another no matter who that other man is and no matter how essential he is to the community. And the evil is even greater when a man sacrifices another innocent man to save himself. Again, I think such religious moral absolutism is mistaken and I shall attempt to show why when I have all our exemplary tales before us.

4. The Mad Matriarch

Consider a not exactly typical group of people living on a small island. (A kind of miniature Haiti, let us say.) Suppose the island is poverty-stricken and very backward and has been dominated for centuries by one dictatorial family. Things in recent years have gone from bad to worse and the island, ruled single-handedly by a mad old matriarch—the last member of the ruling dynasty—is now reduced to starvation and disease. And she is so mad that she cannot be made to understand what is happening to the population on the island and will not release money in her possession that could be used to buy supplies to halt the starvation and enable the island to begin to recover. She is untouchable by the masses of the people for she is thought, as has been believed about the ruling dynasty for as long as anyone can remember, to be a holy witch who can hex anything and destroy at will. It is even almost universally believed by the islanders that to kill her will bring devastation to the island through unleashing the wrath of the evil spirits. Thus her bodyguards remain loyal to her and the population, no matter how bad things get, will not revolt against her. Do not forget that the old woman is not a vicious old woman, just utterly mad. She thinks that by holding on to the money, come what may, she is saving the precious heritage of her land. She cannot be prevailed upon to part with the money, and the population cannot be brought to touch the money while the holy witch lives.

Unless we are to play with words, we should admit that she is an innocent person. After all, she is not responsible for her actions. But suppose you were an intellectual and concerned human being in that country, free from its tribal mythology. What should you try to do? If you hold the kind of normative ethical view I hold and there were no way of saving the starving people other than by killing (murdering, if you will) the old woman, would it not be something you plainly ought to do? I think it is, yet this runs foul of the moral principle of Anscombean Christian absolutism that the direct intention of the death of an innocent person is never justifiable. Again, who is right here? Can anyone be shown to be right or have we come to such fundamental moral differences that we have arrived at differences in moral posture that are unarguable? I think these differences are arguable and that my consequentialist attitude is the right one. In section IV of this chapter I shall turn to that argument.

My exemplary tales so far have been of the kind designed to show that our normal immediate rather absolutist moral reactions need to be questioned along with such principles as 'The direct intention of the death of an innocent person is never justifiable'. I have hinted (and later shall argue) that we should beware of our moral outrage here—our naturally conservative and unreflective moral reactions—for here the consequentialist has a strong case for what I shall call moral radicalism. But before turning to a defense of that, I want to tell three more stories, all taken from Phillipa Foot, but used for my own purposes.[5] These tales, I shall argue, have a different import from our previous tales, for with them I think our unrehearsed, common-sense moral reactions will stand up under moral scrutiny. I shall also argue, when I consider them in section III, that our common-sense moral reactions here, initial expectations to the contrary notwithstanding, can be shown to be justified on consequentialist grounds. The thrust of my argument concerning both sets of cases is that in neither are we justified in opting for a theistic and/or deontological absolutism or in rejecting consequentialism. But to return to our remaining exemplary tales.

5. The Magistrate and the Threatening Mob

A magistrate or judge is faced with a very real threat from a large and uncontrollable mob of rioters demanding a culprit for a crime. Unless the criminal is produced, promptly tried and executed, they will take their own bloody revenge on a much smaller and quite vulnerable section of the community (a kind of frenzied pogrom). The judge knows that the real culprit is unknown and that the authorities do not even have a good clue as to whom he may be. But he also knows that there is within easy reach a disreputable, thoroughly disliked and useless man who, though innocent, could easily be framed so that the mob would be quite convinced that he was guilty and would be pacified if he were promptly executed. Recognizing that he can prevent the occurrence of extensive carnage only by framing some innocent person, the magistrate has him framed, goes through the mockery of a trial and has him executed.

Most of us regard the framing and execution of such a man in such circumstances as totally unacceptable. There are some who would say that it is categorically wrong—morally inexcusable—whatever the circumstances. Indeed, such a case remains a problem for the consequentialist, but here again, I shall argue, one can consistently remain a consequentialist and continue to accept common-sense moral convictions about such matters.

6. The Indispensable Serum

Suppose that several dangerously ill people can be saved only if we kill a certain individual and use his diseased dead body in the preparation of a serum. But we immediately, and, on reflection as well, feel, as Foot observes, that we would not in anything even approximating a realistic situation be justified in killing a man for such purposes. I think that our convictions here are correct, and I shall argue that we can give good consequentialist reasons for sticking by the moral dictates of common-sense morality.[6]

7. The Teleological Torturer

Suppose we have the good fortune to live in a quite open tyranny such as, for example, Iran, Portugal, or South Africa, and that we are faced with a moral dilemma forced on us by the fiendish local representative of the leader. This beastly man presents one of us, as a representative member of the dwindling intelligentsia, with the following (as far as can be discerned) thoroughly earnest proposal: unless we torture one innocent man, our *kleiner Fuehrer* will, with even greater torment than he requires of us, torture five men to death. That is, one member of the intelligentsia is singled out for harassment; unless he tortures one man, five others will be tortured and killed.

If one were the person selected for this harassment, would it not be one's duty, on such an ethical theory as the one I argued for in chapter 5, to torture one man to keep the other five from being tortured to death? I shall argue that it is neither one's duty nor even something that one is morally justified in doing.

My cycle of little moral tales is at an end. The task is to see what they imply. We must try to determine whether thinking through their implications should lead a clear-headed and morally sensitive man to abandon the kind of humanistic and teleological framework I have given to normative ethics and to adopt some form of theistic absolutism and/or deontological absolutism. I shall argue that it does not.

III

I shall consider the last three cases first because there are good reasons for the consequentialist to stick with common-sense moral convictions in such cases. I shall start by giving my rationale for that claim. Consider case 5, the case of the magistrate and the threatening mob. If the magistrate were a tough-minded but morally conscientious utilitarian, he could on straightforward utilitarian grounds refuse to frame and execute the innocent man even knowing that this would unleash the mob (note that in practice it would be very unlikely that he could know that) and cause much suffering and many deaths.

The rationale for his particular moral stand would be that

by so framing and then executing such an innocent man, he would in the long run cause still more suffering, through the resultant corrupting effect on the institution of justice. That is to say, in a case involving such extensive general interest in the issue—without that there would be no problem in preventing the carnage and no call for such extreme measures—knowledge that the man was framed, that the law had prostituted itself, would surely eventually leak out. This would encourage mob action in other circumstances; it would lead to an increased skepticism about the incorruptibility or even the reliability of the judicial process, and it would set a dangerous precedent for less clear-headed or less scrupulously humane magistrates. Given such a potential for the corruption of justice, a utilitarian or consequentialist judge or magistrate could on good utilitarian or consequentialist grounds argue that it was morally wrong to frame an innocent man. If the mob will rampage if such a sacrificial lamb is not provided, then the mob must rampage.

Must a utilitarian or consequentialist come to such a conclusion? The answer is no. It is the conclusion that is, as things stand, the most reasonable conclusion to come to, but that he must come to it is far too strong a claim. A utilitarian could consistently—I did not say successfully—argue that our tough-minded utilitarian magistrate had overestimated the corrupting effects of such judicial railroading. His circumstance was an extreme one, a situation not often to be repeated even if, instead of acting as he did, he had set a precedent by such an act of judicial murder. If that in fact is so, a utilitarian could reason that since very many innocent people would otherwise be murdered and given a firm understanding that this really is the case, the institution of justice would not be extensively harmed at all by such a surreptitious judicial murder. Indeed, a grave injustice with vile consequences would be wrought on one individual, but even worse consequences would follow if the mob were allowed to rampage. Such a utilitarian magistrate would insist that the judicial murder of one innocent man is the lesser evil; and that the lesser evil is always to be preferred to the greater.

The short of it is that utilitarians could disagree, as other consequentialists could disagree, about what is morally required of us in that case. The disagreement here between utilitarians or consequentialists of the same type is not one concerning fundamental moral principles but a disagreement about the empirical facts, about what course of action will in the long run produce the least suffering and the most happiness for everyone involved. (Given the kind of consequentialism I defended in chapter 5, intrinsic goods other than happiness would have to be brought in as well and *everyone's* interests would have to be considered.[7] This would complicate the above statement but would not change the essentials of the dispute. For convenience of expression, but for no other reason, I will continue to put the matter in this utilitarian manner.)

However, considering the effect that advocating the deliberate judicial killing of an innocent man would have on people's reliance on common-sense moral beliefs of such a ubiquitous sort as the belief that the innocent must not be harmed, a utilitarian who defended the centrality of common-sense moral beliefs would indeed have a strong utilitarian case here. But the most crucial thing to recognize is that to regard such judicial bowing to such a threatening mob as unqualifiedly wrong, as morally intolerable, one need not reject utilitarianism and accept some form of theistic or deontological absolutism.

It may be argued that in taking such a stance I still have not squarely faced the absolutist's objection to the judicial railroading of the innocent. I allow, as a consequentialist, that there could be circumstances, at least as far as logical possibilities are concerned, in which such a railroading would be justified but that as things actually go, it is not and probably never in fact will be justified. But the absolutist's point is that in no circumstances, either actual or conceivable, would it be justified. No matter what the consequences, it is unqualifiedly unjustified. To say, as I do, that the situations in which it might be justified are desert-island, esoteric cases that do not occur in life, is not to the point, for, as Alan Donagan argues, "moral theory is *a priori,* as clear-headed utilitarians like Henry Sidgwick recognized. It is, as Leibniz would say, 'true of all possible worlds.' "[8] Thus to argue as I have that the counterexamples directed against consequentialists appeal to conditions that are never in fact fulfilled or are unlikely to be fulfilled is beside the point.[9] Whether a "moral theory is true or false depends on whether its implications for all possible worlds are true. Hence, whether utilitarianism (or consequentialism) is true or false cannot depend on how the actual world is."[10] It is possible to specify logically conceivable situations in which consequentialism would have implications that are monstrous, for example, certain beneficial judicial murders of the innocent (whether they are even more remotely likely to obtain is irrelevant), hence consequentialism must be false.

We should not take such a short way with consequentialists, for what is true in Donagan's claim about moral theory being *a priori* will not refute or even render implausible consequentialism; and what would undermine it in such a claim about the *a priori* nature of moral theory and presumably moral claims is not true. To say that moral theory is *a priori* is probably correct if that means that categorical moral claims—fundamental moral statements—cannot be deduced from empirical statements or nonmoral theological statements such that it is a contradiction to assert the empirical and/or nonmoral theological statements and deny the categorical moral claims or vice versa.[11] In that fundamental sense it is reasonable, and, I believe, justified, to maintain that moral theory is autonomous and *a priori*. It is also *a priori* in the sense that moral statements are not themselves a kind of empirical statement. That is, if I assert "One ought to respect an individual's rights" or "One ought to protect an innocent man," I am not trying to predict or describe what people do or are likely to do, but am asserting what they are to do. It is also true that if a moral statement is true, it holds for all possible worlds in which situations of exactly the sort characterized in the statement obtain. If it is true for one, it is true for all. You cannot consistently say that A ought to do B in situation Y and deny that someone exactly like A in a situation exactly like Y ought to do B.

In these ways moral claims and indeed moral theory are *a priori*. But it is also evident that none of these ways will touch the consequentialist or utilitarian arguments. After all, the utilitarian need not be and typically has not been an ethical naturalist—he need not think moral claims are a subspecies of empirical statement; and he could accept (indeed, he must accept) what is an important truism anyway—that you cannot consistently say that A ought to do B in situation Y and deny that someone exactly like A in a situation exactly like Y ought to do B. But he could and should deny that moral claims are *a priori* in the sense that rational men must or even will make them without regard for the context in which they are made. We say people ought not to exceed the speed limit or speed on icy roads or throw knives at each other. But if human beings had a kind of metallic exoskeleton and would not be hurt, disfigured or seriously inconvenienced by knives sticking in them or by automobile crashes, we would not so evidently at least have good grounds for saying that such speeding or knife-throwing is wrong. It would not be so obviously unreasonable and immoral to do these things if those conditions obtained.

In the very way we choose to describe the situation when we make ethical remarks, it is important in making this choice that we know what the world is like and what human beings are like. Our understanding of the situation, our understanding of human nature and motivation, cannot but affect our structuring of the moral case. Consider the difference between how psychologically secure, knowledgeable persons and uneducated, psychologically insecure persons characterize sexual offenses. What sickens and saddens one man and makes him hope all the more for better conditions of detection and cure of the criminally insane drives another to rage and to demand prompt justice through the use of the death penalty. To recognize and stress the relevance of our knowledge of human nature in the making of moral assessments is perfectly compatible with a recognition, as we find it, for example, in Hume, that moral claims are not empirical claims and that no fundamental moral claim is entailed by an empirical claim.

The consequentialist is saying that, as the world goes, there are good grounds for holding that judicial killings are morally intolerable, though he would have to admit that if the world were very different, they could be something that ought to be done. But in holding this, he is not committed to denying the universalizability of moral judgments, for where he would reverse or qualify the moral judgment, the situation must be different. He is only committed to claiming that where the situation is the same or relevantly similar and the persons are relevantly similar, they must, if they are to act morally, do the same thing. He is claiming that, as things stand, judicial killing of the innocent is always wrong and he is affirming that it is an irrational moral judgment to assert of a reasonably determinate action (for example, killing an innocent man) that it is unjustifiable and morally unacceptable in all possible worlds, whatever the situation and whatever the consequences.

Perhaps such a consequentialist claim with its recognition that we must not make moral judgments without careful attention to context, is in some way mistaken. I am not at all convinced that this is so. On the contrary, it seems to me an important truth about the nature of morality. But whether I am right about this or not, Donagan's claims about the *a priori* nature of moral theories do not show such a claim to be mistaken or even give us the slightest reason for thinking that it is mistaken. What is brutal and vile, for example, throwing a knife at a human being just for the fun of it, would not be so, if human beings were invulnerable to harm from such a direction because they had a metallic exoskeleton. Similarly, what is, as things are, morally intolerable, for example, the judicial killing of the innocent, need not be morally intolerable in all conceivable worlds.

Similar things should be said about case 6, the case of the indispensable serum. Suppose a new kind of deadly plague is raging in Basel, killing people left and right, and that we need to kill a living human who is in a certain stage of the disease to make a serum to halt the plague. Suppose, further, that given the present development of science, this is the only way such a serum could be made. An old man, quite alone in the world and miserable, has contracted the plague and is very likely to die from it and is in the right stage. How can we, given that we are consequentialists and that the plague so virulently stalks the land, deny that we should kill him? A utilitarian, who also remained committed to our common-sense moral convictions about killing innocent people, could reply that the very central importance in morality—including utilitarian morality—of respect for life makes such killing morally unthinkable. As in the case of the magistrate and the threatening mob, respect for justice was at issue, so in the case of the indispensable serum, respect for persons, for life itself, is at issue. We human beings would not want—indeed, could not morally tolerate—a world in which human life and human rights were treated so lightly. We cannot, from a moral point of view, regard a man as a means only. A world in which this was so is not a world in which a moral order prevails and it is not a world in which people could be happy or attain self-fulfillment, so there are very good consequentialist grounds for not preparing a serum—no matter how indispensable—if it is necessary to kill an innocent man to do this.

Again, I do not mean that a consequentialist must accept this particular judgment about serum making but that a consequentialist consistently and plausibly can accept it. Indeed, a consequentialist such as myself who qualified utilitarianism by stressing that it is not enough just to seek maximization of human happiness or satisfaction of desire and minimization of suffering, but that we must maximize and minimize it fairly so that everyone's interests are equally taken into consideration, puts critical weight on the notion of respect for persons. That is what such a qualification of utilitarianism stresses. No one, from a moral point of view, can be left out of account. This is what in essence should be meant by the claim that no one can be treated as a means only.

However, that everyone's interests must be considered does not mean that where there are irreconcilable conflicts of interest, no particular interests should take pride of place. Morality in part exists to give us some means of making a just and humane resolution where there are such conflicts of interest. What it does require is that in moral deliberation, every man's interests must be considered and given an initial equal weight. Departures from the initial positions of equality in the form of special treatment for certain individuals (for example, everything else being equal, a mother with small children rather than an unmarried person should be given first choice for a scarce place in a lifeboat), must be capable of being given general justification (for example, that, everything else being equal, the same thing holds true for anyone who is a mother with small children and for anyone who is unmarried). The resultant positions of inequality (both advantageous and disadvantageous) must be open to all. (By saying that they are open to all, I mean that someone cannot claim them simply on hereditary or racial grounds or, at least for the vast majority of cases, on grounds by which a person by his own good effort could not be in a position to achieve.) Thus, in reasoning morally we must start from a position in which man's interests are to be given equal weight; all subsequent qualifications of this must be fair; that is, they must be in accordance with general principles of justice and equality. Where there are irreconcilable conflicting interests, some sacrifice of interest must be made. The point is to make such necessary sacrifices in as fair and humane a way as possible.

However, even when operating, as I do, from this kind of consequentialist position, one is not *logically* forced, from the weight one gives to the principle of respect for persons, to say that such serum making must be morally intolerable in all conceivable circumstances. Surely the skeptic can ask, how we can be so sure that we—that is, humanity generally—would be happier or would attain greater self-fulfillment in a world made safe from such serum makers? Recall that we say that no man can be treated as a means *only*. When in our situation a man is made serum of, he is not treated as a means *only*. His person is still respected; he is not picked out simply because he is John Jones, a black, poor, conveniently at hand or the like. In fact, in such a situation, one would expect a very moral and very strong man to offer up his life. That he is killed rather than someone else, our skeptical utilitarian will argue, is something having a rationale that, though it sanctions the taking of innocent life, could still be plausibly argued to be just; and there are humane reasons for taking his life rather than someone else's. Is it so evident, when it is carefully thought through, that such a killing of an innocent person is never justifiable? Is it so evident that no logically possible situation could arise in which it would be justified? It is not evident to me that we should answer these questions in the negative.

We very rightly feel utter horror at such a taking of life. But think of the people we allow to die by not killing the man. The usual remark to make here is that we do not intend their death while we deliberately kill the man, and that, it is often said, makes all the difference in the world. There indeed is an important distinction between efforts to avoid harming or killing someone, on the one hand, and bringing aid, on the other. The moral imperative to do the former is normally stronger than the moral imperative to do the latter. No doubt there is always something that someone could do to help save lives somewhere, but this claim of others is not as strong as the claim they have on our forbearing to harm them.

However, while this distinction is a significant one, it is not clear how far it will carry us in considering the present case. If a plague were killing people everywhere and there were no other way of saving vast numbers of people except by such a ghastly serum making, would it then be so evidently wrong to do it? I know well enough, if I had the plague in the right stage, were old and ill (perhaps even if I were not old and ill), and there were no other person or no community in a similar state willing to draw straws, I would feel morally obliged to sacrifice myself. If that is a reasonable moral sentiment and not just an expression of a sick martyr complex and if I am not ill with the plague, but someone else is who fits the description under which I would rightly be prepared to sacrifice myself except that he will not volunteer for the sacrifice, is it so plainly wrong to say that he should be killed?

If we have anything at all approximating moral sensitivity, we reel at the thought of killing someone and there are strong consequentialist reasons against such serum making. If we believe in God, I suppose, it is reasonable to assert "It is all in the hands of God. By not killing, I have harmed no man," and to refrain categorically from such serum making.[12] A secularist, however, cannot so easily escape responsibility. That he cannot and that it is difficult to live with that responsibility is perhaps part of what Nietzsche meant when he said that we must learn to transvaluate values in a world without God. Indeed, it is true that by advocating the killing of someone or by killing someone himself, he wrongly injures that person and perhaps by refraining from action and thus forbearing to prevent many deaths no one is injured by him. No one can justifiably make a claim on the serum-forbearer that he owed him the serum, but still by so acting we who are serum-forbearers are responsible for allowing the plague to rage out of control, among ourselves and our children: the latter being particularly important here for they have no choice in the matter.

Such considerations support the utilitarian or consequentialist skeptical of the claims of our common-sense morality. Yet it may also well be the case—given our extensive cruelty anyway—that, if we ever start sanctioning such behavior, an even greater callousness toward life will develop than the very extensive callousness extant now. Given a normative ethical theory that sanctions such serum-making behavior under certain circumstances, there may occur an undermining of our moral disapproval of killing and our absolutely essential moral principle that all human beings, great and small, are deserving of respect. This is surely enough, together with the not unimportant weight of even our unrehearsed moral feelings, to give strong utilitarian weight here to the dictates of our common-sense morality. Yet I think I have also said enough to show that someone who questions their "unquestionableness" in such a context does not thereby exhibit a "corrupt mind" and that it is an open question whether he must be conceptually confused over this matter if he does not have a "corrupt mind." Still, to put it most conservatively, the consequentialist who remains committed to what I have called a common-sense moral commitment has not been exposed as being inconsistent or somehow confused and vacillating.

The case of the teleological torturer, case 7, can be handled with greater brevity than the case of the indispensable serum for very similar considerations apply in both cases. However, the former merits independent consideration because it reveals a feature of many puzzle-cases that would lead a reasonable consequentialist in considering such cases to defend sticking with common-sense moral convictions. Case 7 was the case where a mad and fiendish tyrant demands that we torture one innocent man or he will torture five men even more fiercely. In this case, consequentialists should absolutely refuse to be teleological torturers and for eminently practical reasons: given a man who is sufficiently mad and morally depraved to make such a demand, we could have no confidence at all that he would stick by his promise and not torture them and others as well after we had done our own horrified torturing to try to lessen the balance of evil resulting from his horrible threat. In such a Caligula-situation, nothing is sufficiently stable to enable us to have even a tolerably steadfast confidence in the tyrant's promises or commitments. Given the enormity of what we are asked to do, given the plain evil and swinishness of it, it is not something the toughest utilitarian would be justified in doing in such a precarious situation. In addition, there are features here that we noted obtained also in the serum case and which strengthen a utilitarian defense of sticking, in such a situation, by our common-sense moral convictions.

It is time now that we look at a reply to what I have been arguing in discussing cases 5, 6 and 7. I shall call it the desert islander argument. Suppose, referring to the case of the teleological torturer, someone says, but what would be the right thing to do if one could be quite confident that our *kleiner Fuehrer* would keep his promise and torture the five others horribly? Suppose there was a precedent here resulting from the fact that the horrible practice had been developed and sustained through the brutal power of the tyranny for some considerable time. Would you not then have good grounds for believing him and then must you not in such a situation, if you care to remain a consistent consequentialist, reluctantly torture to prevent still more evil? Surely it is natural to reply that such monstrous activities, evil in themselves, also have evil side effects: for example, they brutalize one, make one increasingly insensitive to pain, and bring out pervasive latent sadistic impulses that normally are more readily held in check. Such considerations surely strengthen the case for the utilitarian trying to defend common-sense moral convictions, but the determined desert islander can always persist by asking "But what if it would not have such brutalizing side effects?" Must not a consistent consequentialist then become in such a circumstance a teleological torturer?

Suppose we *know* that unless we sawed off a man's arm a tyrant would torture to death a whole town. Should we not then become teleological torturers? Similarly, in response to our utilitarian defense of the case of the magistrate and the threatening mob, the desert islander can ask: "But should not a consistent consequentialist judicially murder such innocent men, when and if he could be perfectly confident that knowledge of it or even rumor of it would not leak out, that it would not have a corrupting effect on him or others and generally that it would not have a corrupting effect on the institution of justice?" And again with the case of the indispensable serum, suppose the situation was very tight: (*a*) the new plague was spreading out from Basel to all of central Europe, (*b*) the killing in such a situation of an innocent man would not so harden one morally or have dangerous political side effects, and (c) that it was quite clear that this was the only way for the next hundred years to make the serum. If this wildly fanciful situation were the real situation, should we not indeed kill him, if we stick by our consequentialist moral principles?

It is indeed true that by heaping on enough conditions the desert islander can always produce a conflict between utilitarianism (or other forms of consequentialism) and certain of our common-sense moral convictions or principles, such as the deep-seated conviction that the direct intention of the death of an innocent person is never justifiable. If we are consequentialists, there are logically possible situations in which we must admit that such behavior would be required of us. But such a possibility, it is argued, is sufficient to discredit such an ethical theory.

There are several things that need to be said about such desert islander arguments. It needs to be carefully noted how unrealistically full of "ifs" the situations are where cases 5, 6, and 7 would produce at least an apparent conflict between our common-sense moral principles and a reflective consequentialism. Moral discourse is fitted for the recurrent practical situations of life and not for such wildly improbable situations as determined desert islanders foist upon us. We might no more know what to say here than we would know what to say in tennis if someone made a very high serve and the ball, without going out of the court, went up and up and we waited two hours and it still had not come down. How are we to count that serve? Is it a fault? The rules were not made to cover such contingencies, such a desert island situation, but there is nothing wrong with them for all that. Similarly in the moral case, in some wildly improbable desert island situations we very well might not know what to say. Moral discourses and moral concepts are none the worse for that.

Such remarks might still be felt to be failing to meet the objection. It is tempting to reply to my above rejection of desert island cases, that nevertheless we understand the conditions and if, *per impossible* if you will, they were to obtain, we can see that on consequentialist principles such swinish acts would be required of us and that they are so evil that they would never be justified or even morally tolerable. This is precisely—

the argument would continue—the value of desert island cases. They bring out what otherwise might be obscured. Thus they are not irrelevant after all.

However, if the desert islander's game is played and we do consider what moral conclusions we should come to about such exotically improbable cases, then we should realize that sticking with the principles of common-sense theistic or deontological absolutism is not so obviously the best or right thing to do. Playing that game we need to take the following desert island cases seriously; and, when we treat them in that way, it is again not obvious that the consequentialist is mistaken. What should we do if it were the case that a whole nation would perish if one innocent man were not murdered, a million innocent people would get killed if a magistrate did not, through fool-proof manipulation, get an innocent man convicted of murder, or a thousand children would be tortured to death if we did not pull out the fingernails of one innocent man? These are all cases, *if* we take them seriously, where it is not at all obvious that we must, on pain of moral error or corruption of mind, stick to absolutistic or Christian deontological principles. If we set aside such desert island cases as irrelevant to moral reflection, as I suggest we should, the consequentialist's position is a strong one. But he is also in a strong position if we nevertheless choose to utilize these cases and really think through what they would involve.

There will indeed be borderline cases that are not quite so "iffy" as the most paradigmatic desert island cases in which, if they were to become real-life situations, we would be in an agonizing moral perplexity. They would be situations in which we would not know what to say or what moral course to take.[13] But that some situations should lead us into such moral surds should not be surprising. Morality is a very complex form of life. There could hardly be a decision procedure here with the precision of the propositional calculus. Moral principles, except, perhaps, such consummately general ones as the principles of utility, justice, and respect for persons, are such that they are tailored to recurrent situations that arise in human living. In such situations, we have good utilitarian and consequentialist grounds for acting in accordance with pervasive common-sense moral dictates of the type discussed.

However, right here, another difficulty becomes evident. It is not unnatural to say that such a contingent defense of such common-sense moral principles is not enough. In discussing the case of the magistrate and the threatening mob and the case of the indispensable serum, I admitted that, depending on their judgments about the empirical facts and the acuteness of their thinking through the implications of their moral postures and their knowledge of men and affairs, conscientious utilitarians and other consequentialists might disagree about what ought to be done in such cases. But if they may so disagree, if a conscientious consequentialist is not forced (logically compelled) to conclude that torturing an innocent person or procuring the judicial execution of the innocent must always be morally intolerable, then—so the objection runs—his position does not give us a sure moral foundation to condemn these things as being morally unthinkable. But, it may be argued, such an assurance is exactly what an adequate morality requires.

We have already seen how Miss Anscombe does not want to argue with such consequentialists, for she concludes from their very taking of such a posture toward the world that they have corrupt minds—that such people have monstrous moral views or are flagrantly disregarding moral considerations. Surely such Christian absolutists want a stronger, more certain foundation for such moral claims than the consequentialist one I gave. That the direct intention of the death of an innocent person is never morally justifiable must remain a closed question for them. To refuse to so treat it, according to them, must be either symptomatic of having an immoral moral code or of going beyond moral considerations altogether.

. Since 'moral' contrasts with both 'immoral' and 'non-moral', there is nothing conceptually inappropriate about speaking of 'an immoral moral code' or of 'an immoral morality'. In so speaking, we are saying that a code that is admittedly a moral code, as opposed to a nonmoral code, is unacceptable because, unlike a morally acceptable moral code, it is an evil, morally intolerable code. Thus someone who regards the sexual habits of the Tahitians as immoral might say consistently enough that Tahitians have an immoral sexual morality; and in Kafka's *Penal Colony,* the explorer gradually comes to understand that the officer has a severe, demanding, and indeed universalizable moral code (he stoically applies it to himself when the occasion arises) containing a commitment to justice while remaining for all that a hideously and unbelievably inhumane morality.

It is not clear whether Christian and deontological absolutists such as Miss Anscombe regard such a consequentialist position as an immoral morality or as some kind of morally sick normative position beyond moral good and evil altogether. It would seem to me more reasonable to argue that it is an immoral morality than to deny that it is a morality at all. In either case, such an absolutism does not have much merit. To say that a consequentialist position is not any kind of moral position at all is surely implicitly to redefine, in a stipulative manner, the way we characterize the difference between a moral and a nonmoral code. But even allowing this linguistic gerry-mandering, nothing is accomplished, for with the narrowed conception of a moral code, the relevant question simply becomes whether, under all conditions, moral considerations should be definitive in determining how we ought to act. Perhaps, it will be queried, in some forms of the extreme situations represented by cases 5, 6, and 7, moral considerations should not be decisive. However, it is less muddling to regard such consequentialist codes as moral codes and to assert that they are immoral codes rather than nonmoral codes. That is to say, this is clearer and less arbitrary linguistically.

The important consideration surely is to get beyond Anscombean dogmatic moral assertion and show how such codes are immoral. It will be argued by all partners to this dispute that it is wrong directly to intend the death of an innocent person and that it is unjust to punish or harm someone for something he did not do or could not help doing. But consequentialists such as myself think that, morally speaking, it is an open question whether in certain very extreme circumstances we should deliberately do what is wrong or unjust to prevent a still greater evil. Or to put it in a less paradoxical way, it is an open question whether in certain extreme circumstances we should not do something that normally would be grossly wrong but is not so evidently wrong here because of the fact that by not doing it a still greater evil is obtained. Surely by giving up a rigid acceptance of the kind of deontological principles such absolutists follow, we have complicated moral decision. But a simpler system that stuck by absolutist principles no matter how much suffering or how much evil resulted would, to put it conservatively, be morally paradoxical. Surely the burden of argument is on such deontologists and Christian absolutists to explain either (a) why one should not always act in accordance with the formula: where faced with two evils both of which cannot be avoided, do the lesser evil, or (b) why it never can be the case that acting unjustly or killing an innocent man is ever in any circumstance the lesser evil. Until such time as a convincing argument is made here, the consequentialist argument appears at least to be very strong and it looks like the Christian absolutist is on a Quixotic and morally irresponsible quest for moral certainty and purity— a quest that will shield him from some very agonizing moral decisions but will hardly enable him to come to grips with some demanding moral dilemmas.

IV

So far, I have tried to show with reference to cases 5, 6, and 7 how consequentialists (including utilitarians) can reasonably square their normative ethical theories with an important range of common-sense moral convictions. Now, by reference to cases 1, 2, 3, and 4, I wish to establish that there is at least a serious question concerning whether such fundamental common-sense moral convictions should always function as moral facts or as a kind of moral ground to test the adequacy of philosophical moral (normative ethical) theories or positions. I want to establish that careful attention to such cases shows that we are not justified in taking the principles embodied in our common-sense moral reasoning about such cases as normative for all moral decisions. That a normative ethical theory is incompatible with some of our moral intuitions (moral feelings or convictions) does not refute the normative ethical theory. What I will try to do here is to establish whether these cases, any more than cases 5, 6, and 7 examined in section III, give us adequate grounds for abandoning the kind of teleological and humanistic normative ethic I argued for in chapter 5 and for adopting some theistic and/or deontological absolutism.

Forget the levity of the example and consider the case of the innocent fat man. If there really is no other way of unsticking our fat man and if plainly, without blasting him out, everyone in the cave will drown, then, innocent or not, he should be blasted out. This indeed overrides the principle that the innocent should never be deliberately killed; but it does not reveal a callousness toward life, for the people involved are caught in a desperate situation in which, if such extreme action is not taken, many lives will be lost and far greater misery will obtain. Moreover, the people who do such a horrible thing or acquiesce in the doing of it are not likely to be rendered more callous about human life and human suffering as a result. Its occurrence will haunt them for the rest of their lives and is as likely as not to make them more, rather than less, morally sensitive. (What is even more likely is that their subsequent behavior will not be substantially affected at all.) It is not even correct to say that such a desperate act shows a lack of respect for persons. We are not treating the fat man merely as a means. The fat man's person—his interests and rights—are not ignored. Killing him is something that is undertaken with the greatest reluctance. It is only when it is quite certain that there is no other way to save the lives of the others that such a violent course of action is justifiably undertaken.

Alan Donagan,[14] arguing rather as Anscombe argues, maintains that "to use any innocent man ill for the sake of some public good is directly to degrade him to being a mere means" and to do this is of course to violate a principle essential to morality and thus to my variety of consequentialism as well. But, as my above remarks show, it need not be the case, and in the above situation it is not the case that in killing such an innocent man we are treating him merely as a means. The action is universalizable, all alternative actions that would save his life are duly considered, the blasting out is done only as a last and desperate resort with the minimum of harshness and indifference to his suffering and the like. It indeed sounds ironical to talk this way, given what is done to him. But if such a terrible situation were to arise, there would always be more or less humane ways of going about one's grim task. And in acting in the more humane ways toward the fat man, as we do what we must do and would have done to ourselves were the roles reversed, we show a respect for his person.[15]

In so treating the fat man—not just to further the public good but to prevent the certain death of a whole group of people (that is, to prevent an even greater evil than his being killed in this way)—the claims of justice are not overridden either, for each individual involved, if he is reasoning correctly, should realize that if he, rather than the fat man, were so stuck, he should in such a situation be blasted out. Thus there is no question of being unfair. And is there really a question of being brutish and inhumane when we consider that by not so acting many people are in effect condemned to death? Surely we must choose between evils here, and where there is no avoiding both and where our actions can determine whether a greater or lesser evil obtains should we not plainly always opt for the lesser evil? And is it not obviously a greater evil that all those other innocent people should suffer and die than that the fat man should suffer and die? Blowing up the fat man is indeed monstrous. But letting him remain stuck while the whole group drowns is still more monstrous.

The consequentialist is on strong moral ground here and if his reflective moral convictions do not square with either certain unrehearsed or certain reflective particular moral convictions of human beings, so much the worse for such common-sense moral convictions. One could even usefully and relevantly adapt an argument of Donagan's here. Consequentialism of the kind I have been arguing for provides so persuasive "a theoretical basis for common morality that when it contradicts some moral intuition, it is natural to suspect that intuition, not theory, is corrupt."[16] Given the comprehensiveness, plausibility and overall rationality of consequentialism, it is not unreasonable to override even a deeply felt moral conviction if it does not square with such a theory, though, if it made nonsense or overrode the bulk of or even a great many of our considered moral convictions, that would be another matter indeed.

The case of the dispensable oldster, case 2, and the case of der Übermensch on a life raft, case 3, take a treatment similar to that of the fat man. In case 2 we surely violate the principle that the direct intention of the death of an innocent person is never justifiable. But where the old man himself is not willing to make the sacrifice that reflective morality requires and where the death of four other younger and very much needed people would result along with his own death, his being forced to go overboard seems to me to be a grim moral necessity. Yet it does violate a moral principle that certain Christian absolutists hold to be a principle that can never be overridden.

In actual practice, morally conscientious people would certainly hold on to the last possible moment and it is necessary in this endeavor to save everyone's life that they should take very considerable risks that might lead to the swamping of the raft and the losing of everyone's life. That consequentialists argue that people must be prepared to take such extreme risks, indicates that, while reasoning as consequentialists here in accordance with the principle of the lesser evil, they have not abandoned the principle of respect for persons or abandoned fairness or acceptance of universalizability. From their moral point of view a desperate effort must be made to save the man's life. And when and if it becomes undeniably evident that all will perish if someone is not sacrificed, the old man is not just selected out arbitrarily. There is a universalizable reason for selecting him rather than someone else and there are humane reasons for it being the sick old man rather than a mother with five small children. Anticonsequentialists often point to the inhumanity of people who will sanction such killing of the innocent, but cannot the compliment be returned by speaking of the even greater inhumanity conjoined with evasiveness of those who will allow even more death and far greater misery and excuse themselves on the ground that they did not intend the death and misery but merely forbore to prevent it? In this context such reasoning and such forbearing to prevent seems to me to constitute a moral evasion. I say it is evasive because rather than steeling himself to do what is morally required here, though in normal circumstances it would be a horrible and vile act, the anticonsequentialist allows, when he has the power to prevent it, a situation that is still many times worse.

In case 3, *der Übermensch* on a life raft, we have a case where I would argue that, morally speaking, it is essential that the cancer-cure genius save himself even if that means he must sacrifice the other innocent man. Note that he is not only willing to kill an innocent man but that, from an Anscombean point of view, he compounds the felony by being willing to kill the innocent to save himself. However, this is a biased characterization of the situation, for he is not willing to kill the innocent man just to save himself; he is willing to save himself at the expense of another man because he has very good reason to believe that he and he alone in the forseeable future holds the key to a solution that will make death from cancer a thing of the past. Moreover, it is not that he denies human rights. He does not think that his life is intrinsically more valuable than the other man's life, but only that it is instrumentally more valuable. Everything else being equal, he has no more right to life than does the other man. But everything else is not equal. One man holds in his hands the key to saving thousands and perhaps millions of lives and untold dreadful suffering while the other does not. Since this is so, it is again a moral necessity rather than a moral monstrosity that this *Übermensch* kill the plain man, if they both cannot be saved and the plain man will not sacrifice himself. (*Übermenschen* of exactly that type in that type of situation must do the same thing.)

My consequentialist reasoning about cases 1, 2, and 3 is often resisted on the grounds that it starts a very dangerous precedent. People rationalize wildly and irrationally in their own favor in such situations. Moreover, it is rarely (if ever) the case that one actually gets a situation even approximating the situation of *der Übermensch* on the life raft. There are very few such genuinely indispensable men, but most people under such duress will come up with ersatz reasons for affording themselves with special treatment. And very frequently if people will put their wits to work or just endure, such admittedly monstrous actions, done to prevent still greater evils, will turn out to be unnecessary. Dudley and Stevens, who made a meal of their cabin boy when adrift at sea without food, were rescued not long after their revolting meal. The general moral principles surrounding bans on killing the innocent are so strong and play such a crucial role in the ever-floundering effort to humanize the savage mind—savage as a primitive and savage again as a contemporary in industrial society—that it is of the utmost social utility, it can be argued, that such bans against killing the innocent not be called into question in any practical manner by consequentialist reasoning.

However, in arguing in this way, my theistic and/or deontological absolutist has now plainly shifted his ground and he
is himself arguing on consequentialist grounds that we must
treat certain nonconsequentialist moral principles as absolute
(as principles that can never in fact, from a reasonable moral
point of view, be overridden, for it would be just too disastrous
to do so). But now he is on my home court and my reply is
that there is no good evidence at all that in the circumstances
I characterized in cases 1, 2, and 3 that overriding these deontological principles would have this disastrous effect. I am aware
that they could set a bad precedent by being extended to other
doubtful cases. But my telling of little stories in some detail
and my contrasting of cases 1, 2, and 3, on the one hand, with
4, 5, 6, and 7, on the other, was done in order to make evident
the type of situation, with its attendant rationale, in which the
overriding of those deontological principles can be seen clearly
to be justified and the type of situation in which this does not
obtain and why. My point was to specify the situations in which
we ought to override our common-sense moral convictions about
those matters as well as the situations in which we are not
so justified or at least it is not clear which course of action
is justified.[17]

If people are able to be sufficiently clear-headed about these
matters, they can see that there are relevant differences between
the two sorts of case. The cases involving rationalization are
quite different from 1, 2, and 3, but it was with these latter
situations where I was (and still am) defending a departure
from the dictates of common-sense morality. But I was also
carefully guarding against extending such moral radicalism,
if such it should be called, to other and more doubtful cases.
Unless solid empirical evidence can be given that such a moral
radicalism, if it were to gain a toehold in the community, would
overflow destructively and inhumanely into the other doubtful
and positively unjustifiable cases, nothing will undermine the
correctness of my consequentialist defense of moral radicalism
in the contexts in which I defended it.

I have tried here by commenting on my seven exemplary
tales to establish that criticisms such as Anscombe's and Donagan's of consequentialism and thus indirectly of the normative
ethic I argued for in chapter 5 were not well taken. Clear-headed

and humane consequentialists will often stick to common-sense moral principles even, when viewed superficially, they appear to be unjustifiable on consequentialist grounds. However, viewed more circumspectly, it is plausible to maintain that they have a consequentialist rationale. (Cases 4, 5, 6, and 7 were of that type.) But there are other situations in which consequentialists should challenge common-sense moral responses and advocate what I call a form of moral radicalism. That is indeed difficult to do, for our own very visceral responses are against it. I feel almost guilty and at least queasy in arguing as I do, as if I were advocating not only something that may indeed contain conceptual blunders (hardly something to feel guilty about) but also something that is morally monstrous or at least perverse. Yet surely the heart should work with the head. We know there are good psychological and moral reasons to have strong feelings about such common-sense moral principles because in the ordinary case they are surely principles to stand by.[18] But we feel equally strongly about unnecessary suffering and choosing the lesser evil. And our heads should tell us that what is morally appropriate in the ordinary case need not be so in the extraordinary case. My argument is that cases 1, 2, and 3 are just those extraordinary cases where we should become moral radicals. In both types of case our considered moral response in the face of the particular moral phenomena is, if it is a rational and humane response, a response which is compatible with and finds an architectonic rationale in my type of consequentialist normative ethic. That is, my moral theory accounts for such moral practices and no convincing grounds have been given for abandoning such a humanism for theistic absolutism or some secular form of deontological absolutism.

V

The foregoing discussion makes it evident that under certain circumstances the concept of morality I have defended commits me to sanctioning and indeed even advocating violence toward certain innocent individuals. I abhor violence as much as any man and I doubly abhor the romanticizing of violence or, as was common in the nineteenth century, the romanticizing of war. It may indeed be true that violence under certain circumstances can be an effective cathartic. It may be for some a "cleansing spirit" or, for some groups of downtrodden people, a way of attaining identity and cohesion. But when I argue that violence, including violence toward the innocent, may under certain circumstances be justified and indeed obligatory, it is not such considerations that prompt me, but the realization that in certain circumstances even greater and more extensive misery will result if violence, and indeed violence toward the innocent, is not accepted, albeit with a heaviness of heart.

To examine this radical claim of mine further and to make good my promissory note to discuss our realistic cases and to anticipate and void the criticism that what I call 'moral radicalism' is only plausible in desert island or quasi desert island situations, I shall discuss some realistic cases.

We spoke in the first section of this chapter of the deliberate bombing of civilian populations and of guerrilla warfare. As actual warfare goes, the deliberate bombings of civilian targets—the bombing of Dresden is a good example—are often senseless and wanton acts of terror in no way justifiable. But consider the bombing in the Second World War of a German residential area housing workers in a strategic munitions factory and keep in mind the need to bring the war to a quick and decisive end in order to halt the slaying and brutalizing of millions of people in concentration camps. The moral case for such bombing seems indeed to be a very strong one. Yet it is plainly (consider the children) violence directed in part against innocent people. To say we do not directly intend their death, if we are acting as moral agents, is indeed true. We want the bombs to kill or injure their parents so as to stop the operation of the munitions factory. (The munitions factory is underground so we cannot bomb it directly.) We do not—and cannot from a humane point of view—want the children to be injured or die. We also know or have very good reason to believe that many children and other wholly innocent people will be killed and yet we deliberately engage in such an action. We are, direct intentions or second intentions or no, overriding the moral principle that one is never justified in killing the innocent. We do it by an appeal to the principle that suffering is evil and that where it cannot be avoided we should choose the lesser suffering. It is true that the innocent in no way deserve to suffer. We cannot rightly speak of their just suffering. In fact, their suffering is unjust. But while justice is a central moral consideration, it is not the only relevant moral consideration and sometimes the claims of justice, where acting on them would cause great misery, should be set aside. In such circumstances, the innocent must suffer undeservedly because, unless they do suffer, a far greater total suffering will ensue.

We should ask those absolutists who say that it is always wrong to inflict suffering on the innocent whether they would be willing to say that it would have been wrong (unjustified and unjustifiable) for the Allies to have followed out the request of the underground and have bombed Auschwitz. By so bombing it, innocent people (some people enslaved in the concentration camps) would have been killed and the bombers would have known or have had every good reason to believe that such people would be killed; but in killing some through the bombing of the grounds, some further thousands of innocent people could have been saved. If this were indeed so—as it seems evident— would it not indeed have been the humane and right thing to do? Or would it have been wrong to have assassinated Hitler— if this was the way one's opportunity came—by throwing a grenade into a crowd where innocent people (including children who were there with their parents) would have been killed as well? To assert that such acts are never morally justifiable, are categorically not to be done is, I submit, to call in question the very humanity (assuming he clearly understood the implications of his position) of such a Christian and/or deontological absolutist. To be such a moral fanatic that one will insist on acting in accordance with such deontological principles, come what may, is to hold a morally monstrous view. It is the implications of such an absolutism that is monstrous and not, as it is too frequently alleged, the implications of a consequentialism that incorporates an independent principle of justice.

NOTES

1. Alan Donagan, "Is There a Credible Form of Utilitarianism?" and H. J. McCloskey, "A Non-Utilitarian Approach to Punishment," in Michael

D. Bayles, (ed.) *Contemporary Utilitarianism* (New York: Anchor Doubleday, 1968).

2. Elizabeth Anscombe, "Modern Moral Philosophy" *Philosophy* (1957): 16-17.

3. Alan Ryan, "Review of Jan Narveson's *Morality and Utility*" *Philosophical Books* 9, no. 3 (1968): 14.

4. In actual life we seldom have the certainty, hypothesized here, about what will happen. How could they be so certain that they would not be rescued or that the loss of one man would make such a difference about capsizing? A recognition of this strengthens the utilitarian case. See T. L. S. Sprigge, "A Utilitarian Reply to Dr. McCloskey," in Michael D. Bayles, (ed.) *Contemporary Utilitarianism* (New York: Anchor Doubleday, 1968).

5. Phillipa Foot, "The Problem of Abortion and the Doctrine of the Double Effect" *The Oxford Review* (Trinity), (1967): 5-15.

6. Later I shall show that there are desert island circumstances—that is, highly improbable situations—in which such serum-making might be a moral necessity. But also I shall show what little force desert island cases have in the articulation and defense of a normative ethical theory.

7. "Everyone" here is used distributively. That is to say, I am talking about the interests of each and every one. In that sense everyone's interests need to be considered.

8. Donagan, op. cit., p. 189.

9. T. L. S. Sprigge argues in such a manner. See Sprigge, op. cit.

10. Donagan, op. cit., p. 194.

11. There is considerable recent literature about whether it is possible to derive moral claims from non-moral claims. See W. D. Hudson, (ed.) *The Is-ought Question* (London: Macmillan, 1969).

12. Elizabeth Anscombe, "Who Is Wronged?" *The Oxford Review* (Trinity), (1967): 16-17.

13. In a neglected but important essay, W. D. Falk has made us keenly aware of what reason can and cannot do about such moral surds. See his "Moral Perplexity," *Ethics* 66 (January 1956).

14. Donagan, op. cit., pp. 199-200.

15. Again, I am not asserting that we would have enough fortitude to assent to it were the roles actually reversed. I am making a conceptual remark about what, as moral beings, we must try to do and not a psychological observation about what we can do.

16. Donagan, op. cit., p. 198.

17. I have spoken, conceding this to the Christian absolutist for the sake of the discussion, as if (1) it is fairly evident what our common-sense moral convictions are here and (2) that they are deontological principles taken to hold no matter what the consequences. But that either (1) or (2) is clearly so seems to me very much open to question.

18. I do not mean to suggest that I am giving a blanket defense of our common-sense morality. That is one of the last things I would want to do. Much of what we or any other tribe take to be common-sense morality is little better than a set of magical charms to deal with our social environment. But I was defending the importance of such cross-culturally ubiquitous moral principles as 'one ought not to harm the innocent' or 'promises ought to be kept'. However, against Christian absolutists of the type I have been discussing, I take them to be *prima facie* obligations. This means that they

always hold *ceteris paribus;* but the *ceteris paribus* qualification implies that they can be overridden on occasion. On my account, appeal to consequences and considerations of justice and respect for persons determines on which occasions they may be overridden.

7

Hobbesist and Humean Alternatives
to a Religious Morality

I

In his *Letter Concerning Toleration* John Locke remarked,
". . . those are not at all to be tolerated who deny the being
of a God. Promises, covenants, and oaths, which are the bonds
of human society, can have no hold upon an atheist. The taking
away of God, though but even in thought, dissolves all."[1] When
we read this now, we feel the cultural distance between ourselves
and the seventeenth century. Even such a progressive and
reasonable thinker as Locke is, in this respect, at a very great
distance from us. There are in North America Neanderthal
undercurrents, indeed at present very vocal and powerful undercurrents, that still think in this way, but among the intelligentsia, both religious and nonreligious, such thinking is
totally alien. David Gauthier commenting on this passage from
Locke remarks:

> The supposition that moral conventions depend on religious
> belief has become alien to our way of thinking. Modern moral
> philosophers do not meet it with vigorous denials or refutations;

From the *International Journal for Philosophy of Religion* 14 (1983): 33–47.
Reprinted by permission of the publisher.

usually they ignore it. If the dependence of moral conventions on religious belief was necessary for Locke, it is almost inconceivable to us.[2]

Is this just a shift in the *Weltgeist* or does it have rhyme or reason? Does the taking away of God or the thought of God—the sincere belief in His existence—dissolve all as Locke thought? If it does, that would indeed, to understate the matter, make belief in God very central to any acceptance of morality. But is there such a dissolution such that belief in God has such a central place?

Suppose we try to say that it is God's commanding or ordaining something that makes something good. Without His ordaining it, it is claimed, it could not correctly be said to be good. There is no goodness without the commandments of God. Indeed it is the very reality of its being commanded by God that constitutes its goodness.

However, this plainly could not be true, because even in a Godless world kindness still would be a good thing and the torturing of little children could still be vile. Even if we do believe in God, we would still recognize, if we will reflect on the matter and if we have any moral understanding at all, that such acts, even if God does not exist, are wrong and that kindness and decency are good. Reflective people who believe in God and have an ordinary pre-theoretical understanding of morality will come to recognize, if the matter is put to them forcefully, that even if there were no God, torturing people just for the fun of it still would be intolerable. Moreover, the religious believer himself will appreciate, if he carefully reflects, that even if that in which he places his trust and on which he sets his heart, did not exist, keeping faith with his friends would still be a good thing and caring for his children would still be something that he ought to do.

So the goodness or badness, the moral appropriateness or inappropriateness of these acts cannot be constituted by their being commanded by God or ordained by God. Certain moral realities would remain just as intact in a Godless world as in a world with God.[3]

To the old conundrum "Is something commanded by God because it is good or is it good because God commands it?"

it should be responded that whatever way the religious moralist goes, here he is in trouble. On the one hand, that God commands something doesn't *ipso facto* make it good. We can come to appreciate this, if we examine reasonably closely our own considered convictions. If God, just like that, commands us to starve our children that doesn't, just because God so commanded it, make it morally tolerable, let alone good. On the other hand, if God commands something *because* it is good, then plainly goodness stands in logical and moral independence of God.

Have I not missed, in arguing as I have, the perfectly evident consideration that if the God of Judeo-Christianity exists, then everything is dependent on Him: He created the world and everything in it. Moral realities, like everything else, are dependent on Him.

God, let us for the moment assume, did create the world, but He could not—logically could not—create moral values. Existence is one thing; value another. And it is no contravention of God's omnipotence to point out that He cannot do what is *logically* impossible. Moreover, to try to counter by asserting that nothing would be good or bad, right or wrong, if nothing existed, is not to deny that we can come to understand, without reference to God, that it is wrong to exploit people in underdeveloped countries and that religious tolerance is a good thing. The religious moralist has not shown that such exploitation would be wrong and that such tolerance would not be good even if the atheist were right and God did not exist.

If the stance of the religious apologist is to be made out, he must give us some reasonable grounds for believing that in a world without God nothing could be good or bad or right or wrong. If there is no reason to believe that torturing little children would cease to be bad in a Godless world, we have no reason to believe that, in any important sense, morality is dependent on religion. But God or no God, religion or no religion, it is still wrong to inflict pain on helpless infants when inflicting pain on them is without any rational point. John Locke, whatever anxieties he may have felt about Thomas Hobbes's anthropocentric viewpoint, is mistaken: the taking away of God does not dissolve all.

II

I think the above is sufficient to block the refrain: "Without God, no morality, everything is permitted." Still—there always seems to be a "still"—there are those who will think, or at least ambivalently worry, that, with my appeal to considered judgments (convictions), I have exhibited no rational foundation for morality and have, in effect, left a vacuum that theology can fill. Morality, if we resist that and go my roughly Humean way, must finally rest, some believe, on commitment and thus, or so the claim goes, there is no escaping a certain arbitrariness in morality and in the living of our lives.

I think such remarks about 'arbitrariness' are in certain respects thoroughly mistaken or, at the very least, misleading.[4] Still, even if we are willing to talk that way, we can and should respond: even if morality finally rests, in some sense yet to be specified, on commitment, still not all commitments need be arbitrary or without point or rationale. Moreover, this, if such a remark about the nature of morality is correct, is as unavoidable for the religious moralist as for the secular moralist. But, in addition, we should also recall, the secular moralist need not attach to his conception of morality and the moral life a cosmology of dubious coherence and he need not crucify his intellect with an obscurantist mythology.

There is, however, among secular moralists—indeed among secular humanists—a divide between those coming out of a more broadly speaking Humean tradition and those coming out of a broadly speaking Hobbesist tradition. The Humeans are acutely aware of the Wittgensteinian aperçu: "Justification must come to an end or it wouldn't be justification," "It is difficult to realize the extent of our groundless believing," "At the foundation of well-founded belief lies belief that is not founded," "Not everything we reasonably believe we believe for a reason."[5] They believe—to say they see or they acknowledge would be to beg the question—that in an important way morality, secular as well as religious, rests on commitment: rests on what Hume came to call "the sentiment of humanity." The Hobbesists, by contrast, are much more rationalistic: morality, in an important way, is grounded in reason. We can, if we keep our nerve and lower somewhat our expectations, clear-headedly and tough-mindedly bargain our way into morality. David Gauthier and Kurt Baier are the two leading contemporary Hobbesists.[6] I think we have much to learn from them and they go a long way toward giving us the foundations of a secular morality. I want, by stating and examining some core arguments in Kurt Baier's work, to show what some of this is and then indicate why the less rationalistic, broadly, Humean approach is closer to the mark, is, if you will, a better underpinning for a humanistic ethic, if indeed such an underpinning is needed.

III

Kurt Baier proceeds in a very literal and very commonsensical manner to consider some very central moral questions. In doing this, Baier has tried to bypass many of the stock questions of ethical theory and he has tried, while remaining rigorously analytical, to provide an objective and rational answer to fundamental justificatory questions in ethics. He has tried to establish that there are objective and rational principles of moral assessment—principles that can be seen to hold quite independently of the attitudes that moral agents have or the decisions of principle they are willing to make.

I shall principally examine here his "popular" essay "Meaning and Morals."[7] There some of his central claims and assumptions stand out starkly. Baier does not maintain that he is making meta-ethical remarks about "the logic of moral discourse." In fact he doesn't adopt that tone of voice at all. He refers to the account of morality he is elucidating and defending as "a humanist ethics," which he contrasts with the conventional morality embedded in a Judeo-Christian view of things. He maintains for "the ideal of morality" he has sketched that its "greatest merit" is "its capacity to generate an unchallengeable method for determining what is morally right and wrong."[8]

> Unlike other theories, this theory does not have to base its method for determining what is right and wrong on the generally accepted views of what is so. It does not have to plead for creditability by the proof that its results will be

acceptable to all right-thinking men. On the contrary, it
determines who the right-thinking men are, and what are
sound and what are unsound moral convictions in a given
community. For this theory starts from an explanation of why
a certain sort of modification of the precepts of egoism is
necessary for the best possible life for everyone, and why these
necessary modifications must have the status of categorical
imperatives, that is, of absolutely binding obligations. Such
an explanation provides a justification for a system of such
modifications, and so also for the precepts constituting such
a system.⁹

These are indeed claims of considerable scope and while
the *manner* is in certain respects, like the *manner* of Ross or
Broad, the *matter*—the actual underlying claim—is, *vis-à-vis*
contemporary ethical theory, as revolutionary as is Nietzsche's
or Stirner's claims about morality. For a philosophical theory
to generate "an unchallengeable method for determining what
is morally right and wrong" so that by using it we could
determine "who the right-thinking men are, and what are sound
and what are unsound moral convictions in a given community"
is indeed, to put it minimally, a very considerable accomplish-
ment. And the claim that this could be achieved is a very strong
claim indeed. In the face of a pervasive, though often rather
inarticulate, acceptance of relativism or skepticism over values,
Baier's claim is a very radical one. It would, if justified, at last
provide the holy grail that moralists have long sought, and
indeed would accomplish things that most contemporary moral
philosophers think are beyond the competence of moral
philosophy or for that matter any discipline or cluster of dis-
ciplines to achieve. We should look upon Baier's claims both
with considerable interest and with considerable suspicion.

By way of clearing the decks, Baier makes the negative
point that it is theistic religious beliefs, including often a belief
in a heaven of rewards and sometimes even a hell, that are
the *sanctions* that *cause* many people in our culture to accept
the conventional morality of our group. But such religious views
are now discredited, and the question immediately arises why
then continue to accept the conventional morality? And indeed
much of conventional morality has come under a well-grounded

suspicion. Parts of it have received even an outright rejection by many people. But the very tottering quality of the pillars of conventional morality, provokes, in the absence of a clearly articulated and plausibly defended moral alternative, a characteristic nihilistic or skeptical *malaise*. All moral claims come under suspicion. And this is just what has happened. Running against the stream, Baier wants to demonstrate that that wholesale skepticism is unjustified.

There are, of course, antiskeptical moves that plainly won't wash. Baier, not atypically, regards such alleged objective standards as "the voice of conscience," "the moral sense" or the claims of intuition as only the "dressed up demands of our society."[10] That is to say, they simply reflect the standards of our conventional morality; they do not afford a rational and objective basis for morality. They "cannot tell us what is right and what is wrong in a sense which provides an adequate reason for doing what is right and refraining from doing what is wrong."[11]

So far Baier's remarks have been negative; he has only told us how we cannot ascertain what is really right as distinct from what is mistakenly thought to be so. We want, he stresses, to be able to distinguish, what is, on the one hand, known or reasonably believed to be right from what, on the other hand, is merely *felt* to be right. Baier argues that since we cannot rely on intuition to do this and since we cannot rely on how people, neither sophisticates nor the plainest of plain people, feel, we must, to give a theoretical account of our moral knowledge, "base our knowledge of right and wrong on some form of calculation."[12] Here he, like Gauthier, shows a clear indebtedness to Hobbes.

Among the classical normative ethical accounts, egoism— that is what many contemporary philosophers have called 'ethical egoism'—and utilitarianism are both such calculative accounts. Baier rejects both and proposes an alternative calculative moral theory.

We should first see why Baier believes that egoism is, as he puts it, open to a "completely decisive objection" and how Baier's own account, keeping what is true and important in the precepts of egoism, "gives egoism a certain sort of modification which will give us the substructure of a true morality," i.e., an ideal of morality that is internally consistent, coherently elaborated and rationally validated.

To see what this "true morality" could be, we need to see why egoism needs modification. By 'egoism' Baier means, and I shall mean, the view that "each individual can tell what it would be right for him to do by calculating what would be in his best interest."[13]

The decisive objection to this account of right and wrong, according to Baier, is that *if* everybody accepts 'ethical egoism' the result will be "wholly undesirable," yet to count as a moral ideal or even as an account of morality at all, it must be an account that "must hold for everyone." But if ethical egoism is everyone's ideal—if it is to hold for everybody and if it is to be taken to be a mandatory ideal of conduct for everybody (as it must to be a moral ideal)—then it will be a very undesirable ideal indeed and thus we have as sound a reason as we can ask for, for rejecting egoism as a candidate moral system.

Why exactly will the result be wholly undesirable, if *everybody* accepts 'ethical egoism' as an ideal of conduct? The answer is to be found in the following considerations. As a matter of fact, as things stand now and are going to stand in any even tolerably realistic social context, "the best interests of one person often conflict with the best interests of another."[14] This is not a logical necessity or some kind of conceptual necessity (assuming in an anti-Quinean spirit we go in for conceptual necessities), but it is something that will repeatedly happen in any society, though plainly more in some societies than others. So being in a situation where human interests frequently conflict, the ethical egoist has to say that each person would find out what is right for him to do by calculating what would be in his best interest and that this is something *everyone* ought to do. But since the best interests of one person often conflict with the best interests of another, if a person *succeeds* in promoting his own best interests, if he actually is able to do what, given the truth of ethical egoism, he ought to succeed in doing, he "will thereby often *prevent* another agent from promoting his (that agent's) own best interest."[15] As Baier nicely puts it:

> In such a situation, the competitors will often waste much ingenuity and effort on getting the better of each other, perhaps

in the process even harm each other, without in the end being able to accomplish more than they would have accomplished if they had abandoned their efforts to gain an advantage for themselves and had settled the conflict by tossing a coin; and frequently they will accomplish less. As a universal method of determining what each person *should* do, egoism is not therefore the best policy. In social contexts such a mode of behavior does not yield the results it was ostensibly designed to yield: the greatest possible good for each person.[16]

If not ethical egoism, then what moral principles do count as rational principles of behavior that can justifiably *be recommended to everybody?* We need, Baier argues, a principle, or set of principles, which, if acted on, would most likely lead, of all the alternatives, to the *successful promotion* of the interests of each and "through it the best possible life for each."[17] We should adopt those principles of behavior and rules of conduct which would, if adopted, provide *"the best possible life for everyone."*[18] They are the principles and rules that can recommend themselves to all reasonable men. And it is an emotional truism "that the best possible life for everybody cannot be achieved in isolation but only in social contexts in which the pursuits of each infringe on the pursuits of others."[19] If we carefully reflect on this empirical truism, we should come to recognize that the "single-minded pursuit of one's own best interest, irrespective of how it affects others, cannot be the supreme rational principle of behavior."[20] What should be sought instead is the achievement of the maximum satisfaction of interest for *everyone*. With this stress on the maximum satisfaction of interests we capture what is important and valuable about utilitarianism and with the stress on *everyone* being treated alike, we capture the distributive rationale of justice as fairness: something that goes beyond utilitarianism. But in accepting such a principle as the supreme rational principle of conduct, we need not and should not abandon the pursuit of self-interest—as long as it is not an exclusive pursuit of self-interest come what may—for each person is usually the best judge of his own interests and the satisfaction of the interests of everyone is best attained, Baier claims, by each person normally acting in accordance with his own rational interests. However, in those situations, where, by so acting, his behavior, more than some other alternative, would interfere with the maximum satisfaction of interest for everyone, i.e., the best possible life for everyone, then in such situations his self-interested behavior must be constrained. That is to say, egoistic behavior must—morally must—be prohibited in such circumstances. This is as true for a humanistic morality as for a religious morality.

In trying to determine what is a good reason for doing something, we should start, Baier argues, from an egoistic basis, for that something is in our interest is plainly a good reason for doing it if anything is. But while this is our starting point, it need not be, and indeed should not be, our end point, for we have seen that certain other reasons can override in certain contexts purely self-interested considerations.

In recognizing that we have to adopt general modifications of the principles of egoism for purposes "of attaining the best possible life for everybody," we need to determine what characteristics a morality so modified will have. Such a morality will have four distinct features.

(1) Its precepts should be capable of coming into conflict with the precepts of self-interest.

(2) Its precepts should be thought of as overriding those of self-interest.

(3) Each man should have an interest in other people being moral because other people's immorality will tend to affect the achievement of his own rational interests.

(4) Each person should have an interest in the effective enforcement of the principles and precepts of morality.

The advantage to us of restricting the general occurrence of utterly egoistic policies of action is patent. Even a tolerably reasonable group of interacting self-interested individuals can readily be brought to see that they "can improve their lives by adhering to certain restrictions on the precepts of egoism."[21] Such agents should have an interest in the effective enforcement of the principles and precepts of morality and, in particular, they should—even viewing the matter in a coldly rational way—have a general interest in seeing to it that moral considerations override conflicting, purely selfish considerations. To aid in the effective continuance of the institution of morality, a rational self-seeker should be prepared "to pay his share of the price of improvement in life for all, but only," Baier argues, "if the others are prepared to pay their share."[22] Still he very much needs to recognize that his "decision to curb his own egoistic behavior does not make it the case that others will act the same way." It is, therefore, in his interest to support a social device that would ensure that his sacrifice is paralleled by that of others. The enforcement of social rules by various forms of social sanctions is such a device. If effective, such social sanctions ensure that in cases of conflict members of the social order will follow the sanctioned rules rather than the rules of self-interest. In a perfect society—a society in which the ideal of a rational morality obtained—"everyone could be sure that by following the moral principles and precepts he would contribute his necessary share of the price of the best possible life."[23]

In an ideal moral order there would be such a complete coincidence of morality and self-interest. In such an order the sanctions would be such that no one would find it worthwhile to allow selfish considerations to override moral ones. One could rest secure that by curbing one's selfish impulses, where they conflict with the dictates of morality, one was not being "a sucker," for others would do likewise. The agent, in such an ideal order, while still acting in accordance with a morality whose principles override the principles of self-interest, could aim at the best possible life for himself; for the best possible life in such an ideal moral order would not be one in which his selfish interests were allowed to override the dictates of such a rational morality. The best possible life plainly can only be lived in society. A morally unrestrained pursuit of the best possible life for oneself, no matter what the consequences for others, leads to what Hobbes called "the war of all against all" and this state, Baier points out, falls "far short of the best possible life."[24] This can be seen even in self-interested terms.

An underlying and very fundamental rational goal of any rational individual is to obtain the best possible life. This Baier takes to be a truism. On Baier's humanist view of morality, both the precepts of self-interest and morality are guidelines to that goal. They are rival guidelines for the individual. But, where they are construed as guidelines for the best possible life for *all*, it is a sound morality that actually is a correct rational guideline for the best possible life for every individual.

A humanistic ethic and egoism differ in that the "precepts of self-interest formulate guidelines designed in such a way that an individual following them thereby promotes his own interest, regardless of how that affects others."[25] By contrast, "the precepts of morality formulate guidelines designed in such a way that an individual following them promotes the advantage of another, and that all those governed by a given morality derive the greatest possible advantage if *all* follow these guidelines."[26] The point is that everyone will be better off, if everyone follows these moral guidelines by placing curbs on their exclusively self-interested orientations.

Beyond that, Baier claims, his humanistic account of morality can explain why "basic moral precepts are regarded as obligatory, i.e., *absolutely* binding and why there is a telling and decisive answer, whatever one's attitude may be, to the question 'Why should one be moral?' "[27] The answer, Baier claims, is *not* that one should be moral if one happens to desire the greatest good for the greatest number or because one happens to care for others, but that one should be moral because by being moral a person "contributes his share to the best possible life for all, always including himself."[28] Certain fundamental moral precepts are taken to be obligatory because, unlike purely self-interested precepts, it is in other people's interests and not merely in the agent's interest that he act in accordance with them. If the agent allows self-love to override moral considerations, other people's interests are deeply affected and, because of this, one is justified in instituting adequate sanctions to compel the agent to act in accordance with moral precepts. Thus such basic moral precepts are rightly regarded not merely as something that it is desirable to act in accordance with, but also as precepts that are obligatory, i.e., principles that are justifiably enforced and not left to an individual's own discretion. One is not at liberty, either to act in accordance with the moral point of view or not to act in accordance with the moral point of view. For one is simply *obliged* to act in accordance with the moral point of view. One *must* do one's best to be fair and to contribute one's share to the best possible life for all. These are obligations that are *categorical* and Baier, without making a mystery, can, he claims, account for their categoricalness. They are categorical because their being generally observed is absolutely essential for the existence of a moral community and such a community is essential to prevent life from being an unbridled clash of rival egoisms in which there is a "war of all against all." People can not attain the best life for everyone unless moral precepts are taken as overriding the precepts of self-interest.

In trying to decide which principles are to be the substantive moral principles of such a morality, we should look for those principles that we would take as crucial in deciding what to do in determining the best possible life for everyone, when we are faced with situations in which success by one person in the pursuit of his interests would mean failure by another in pursuit of his.

IV

Everything, however, may not be such clear sailing. Why should a rational self-seeker be prepared, where he can rely on others acting as persons of principle, to pay his share of the price for the improvement of life when his failing to do so will be undetected and will not materially affect others continuing to pay their own share? To do so, to do one's own share, is plainly only to be fair. Morality can require no less of him. And perhaps he will, on reflection, just *want* to be fair or perhaps he will find himself *committed* to acting fairly or come to so *commit* himself. But suppose he does not. Can we show that he is thereby behaving less rationally or with less intelligence than the chaps who do? In acting so unfairly he is clearly acting immorally. But what if he only cares about, as far as his own actions are concerned, the semblance of morality and nothing for its reality? Must he thereby be less exactly informed or make more inductive or deductive mistakes or attend less adequately to his own interests than his moralist counterpart? There is no sound argument for believing that anything like this need be so. We have no good grounds for thinking an immoralist *must* be an irrationalist or even less rational than the reflective person of moral principle.

Why, looked at from an individual agent's point of view, would the prudent pursuit of one's own interest, when *not* many others are doing likewise, even when some considerable number of others are harmed, lead to a Hobbesian "war of all against all"? We have no good reason to believe that this would actually be the result. An individual need not, indeed should not, advocate such prudent self-seeking for everyone but, all the same, he can take it as something a reasonable, throughly self-interested person might very well do for himself, provided not too many others had adopted or would adopt that personal policy. Baier claims such a personal advocacy is mistaken, indeed even irrational. But, how can it be shown, or can it be shown, that this is so?[29]

It is, indeed, true that if we all curb self-interest in certain contexts and follow the dictates of a rational morality, then *all* (taken *collectively*) obtain a greater advantage than if we all, or even many of us, act exclusively from self-interest. But this greater advantage need not obtain for a solitary individual or individuals—that is for all taken *distributively*—for such an individual or a few individuals might very well attain the greatest possible advantage if they, in certain circumstances, prudently ignored moral considerations and if all others or most others stuck to them. Where someone could do this with sufficient discretion so as not to destabilize the extant morality, why shouldn't he so act in such circumstances? What is irrational or even unreasonable about it? Baier claims that such an individual is being irrational or unreasonable, but what are his grounds? Unless he gives 'irrational'/'rational' or 'reasonable'/'unreasonable' a question-begging moral reading, it would appear that he has no good grounds for such a claim.

V

These general conclusions are reinforced and deepened by examining Hume's remarks about justice and the "sensible knave."

The practices of justice, which for Hume rest on conventions, would, Hume believes, be stable if people were really guided by their overall interests. But, Hume also believes, if we look at matters from an *individual's* point of view, we should come to recognize that "a man may often seem to be a loser by his integrity."[30] This, of course, does not gainsay the fact that for a society to exist there must be institutions of justice, and for human life to flourish these institutions must be strong. Even what Hume calls a "sensible knave," or what we would now call a thoroughly rational but unprincipled bastard, will be for the strengthening of such moral institutions. Such institutions, he will recognize, are for our mutual benefit. But a sensible knave, "in *particular incidents,* may think that an act of iniquity or infidelity will make a considerable addition to his fortune, without causing any considerable breach in the social union."[31] "That honesty is the best policy," Hume remarks, "may be a good general rule, but is liable to many exceptions; and it may be thought, such a sensible knave conducts himself with most wisdom, if, while observing the general rule, he takes discreet advantage of all exceptions."[32] Each person, if he is thoroughly rational, prefers *universal* conformity to the dictates of justice to the expected outcome of general nonconformity to such dictates, but, at least some rational persons, i.e., sensible knaves, prefer, *in some particular situations,* not to conform to such dictates even if others conform. We can put this general point in an even stronger way, as David Gauthier does, "Each expects to benefit from the just behavior of others, but to lose from his own, hence, whenever his own injustice will neither set an example to others, nor bring punishment on himself, his interests will dictate that injustice."[33] Hume believes that there is no way of proving the sensible knave mistaken. There is no sound argument that shows that such a knave must be irrational or that he acts against reason or even, by contrast with the person of moral principle, that his rationality is diminished.

Hume, however, also believes, in a manner perfectly compatible with what I have just said, that, since the outcomes of *general* conformity are rationally preferred to the outcomes of *general* nonconformity, there is a moral obligation to conform to the dictates of justice. Looked at *not* from an individual's point of view in an *agent-relative* manner but generally in an *agent-neutral* manner, it will be evident that that is so. Experience and reflection show us the "pernicious effects," to use Hume's words, of general or even extensive nonconformity. In this respect Hume does not differ from Hobbes and contemporary Hobbesists. A recognition of the pernicious effects of such nonconformity will check in rational people their inclination to nonconformity to the requirements of justice, where they see the possibility of that way of acting being socially catching. Indeed, they will come to see conformity in such circumstances as obligatory. Both this obligation, as well as the individual's inclination not to be just, rest on interests. The obligation is not, as Baier believes, categorical. It is not, that is, something an agent *must* will if he is rational. Yet each of us has an interest in seeing that the rules of justice are maintained. But it is also the case that each of us, *as individuals*, as the sensible knave makes evident, has an interest "in taking advantage of 'the exceptions'—in violating the rules of justice when violation would go uncopied and unpunished."[34]

What is important to recognize here is that we have reasons, as far as our individual conduct is concerned, for, in certain circumstances, engaging in a discreet neglect of what is required of us morally and that we have, as well, reasons for sticking in all circumstances with what is required of us morally. As rational agents, we will want a society in which people generally do what they acknowledge is morally required of them. But each of us, for ourselves as individuals, will see that, where we can get away with it, it very well could be the case that in certain circumstances it is in our rational self-interest to act, as a free-rider, against our own moral integrity. Perhaps these situations are much rarer than we at first blush are inclined to think; they may even be desert-islandish situations, but they show that there is nothing conceptually untoward about being such a sensible knave or nothing intrinsically irrational.

It has been argued that in spite of this it is Hume's considered belief that a thoroughly rational agent will stick with the moral point of view—will endeavor to do what morality requires of him. Whatever Hume may have thought, it is my belief that this is a comforting tale moral philosophers tell themselves. I do not think that Hume or anyone else has shown that Hume's sensible knave must suffer from a rational defect. That he suffers from a *moral* defect is perhaps tautological, but tautological or not, it is certainly evident enough. But his suffering from a moral defect is one thing, his suffering from a rational defect is another. My point is that he need not be irrational. It may be that "a moral system, being an ideal of conduct, is based on principles that must be accepted by reason . . . ."[35] That would only warrant the claim that these principles are *consistent* with reason. Still, if we will reflect on how our sensible knave might act, we will come to see that these principles are not, for an individual in certain circumstances, *required* by reason. Immorality need not be a species of irrationality.

VI

I think we can see here an important way in which the Humean wins over the Hobbesist as well as over the Kantian. When looked at from the point of view of an individual agent deliberating about how she/he is to live, reason does not require morality, though this is not to say that to choose morality— to seek to be and remain a person of moral principle—is in any way irrational or rationally untoward, requiring someone to be a knight of faith. Morality is *compatible* with reason even though it is not *required* by it. An unprincipled person, as we have seen, need not be irrational. Moreover, sentiment *need* not conflict with reason. A 'rational sentiment' is not a contradiction in terms and an 'irrational sentiment' is not a pleonasm. But this, broadly speaking, Humean view does show that a secular morality, in setting itself against religious obscurantism, should not try to root itself in an ethical rationalism. But a recognition of this should not lead us to a disdain of reason or to a general setting of reason and sentiment into dubious battle. They can conflict but they need not and they do not in any general, conceptually required way. We can see, from following out Baier's argument, how far a conception of the function of morality, plus a clear, cold conception of rationality as calculation, can carry us in rationalizing life: in making sense of our commitment to morality. But we can also see how, finally, morality does rest on a commitment, but this is no less so for the religious person than the secular. There are no axioms of pure practical reason on which to ground morality. Such a Kantian project is not in the cards. There is no overall normative ethical system with derived middle level rules for practical life that is required by reason. But a nonevasive reflection on that should not drive us to religion to make sense of morality, of our moral commitments, and of our tangled lives.

VII

Nothing that I have argued previously should be taken to gainsay the fact that religious moralities with their linked cosmologies do give us a comprehensive picture—some might even call it a theory—about the way the world is and a connected set of moral recipes for living our lives, definite rules for what to do and what not to do, nicely arranged in a hierarchy. Catholic and Anglican doctrines of the natural moral law are paradigmatic here. Such a theory of morality undergirding what was once a shared common morality has long, at least among the educated elites (both nonreligious and religious), been on the decline. And, across almost all sectors of the society, there is a slow but steady falling apart of a once-common morality wedded to a cluster of sister religions, i.e., Judaism, Christianity, and Islam, where authority was once pervasively acknowledged. This erosion has left a cultural void, and, with some people, including not a few philosophers, a nostalgia for the Absolute.

Ethical rationalism, even if it could somehow be defended intellectually, cannot fill that void. There is something rather pitiful in the naive otherworldly utopianism of the moral philosopher who thinks we can develop a systematic moral theory in which, without a sociology with an empirically grounded theory of human nature, the moral precepts do all the work. Without such a set of background beliefs, giving them content and placement, even the systematic arrangement of such precepts does not provide such a grounding for the moral life. Moreover, it is a dream of an otherworldly spirit-seer to think that a theory of morality can be constituted and rationally defended in which we have a system of moral laws and precepts, binding on all rational creatures, with a form and a content that all normal humans, if only they will study it closely, will acknowledge is simply required by reason. A secular morality need not and should not seek to ground itself in such a pale imitation of the old religious moralities. With the death of God, we should not, seeking a substitute, make a God of a reified conception of Reason. We neither can get nor do we need such systems of general principles and truths as ethical rationalism tenders. We do not need, and indeed cannot have, such an appeal to pure practical reason to back up morality or to reconstitute something of a lost shared morality. Our social world would have to change rather extensively for a shared morality to extend much beyond a few moral truisms—truisms that it could nonetheless be worthwhile to assert in certain social contexts.[36]

I have argued that to make sense of our moral lives we do not need to try to make reason, divorced from sentiment and an appeal to our considered judgments in wide reflective equilibrium, authoritative for morality. If we are informed about our social world—if we have some sense of who we are, how we got to be who we are and some reasonable understanding of the options for our collective future—and if we are cool-headed, and if we exercise our capacities for impartial reflection, we can trust our moral sentiments perfectly well in the absence of such grandiose normative ethical theories. None of us are quite such paragons of reflective intelligence as was described above, but we can, in varying degrees, approximate that condition. We need neither God nor moral theory to make sense of our lives. We can have a sensible morality without moral philosophy. That the making sense of our lives eludes so many of us is not because God is dead and we are without a systematic ethical theory of the Kant/Sidgwick variety. Our *malaise* has to do not with that, but essentially with the condition of our lives as social beings: it essentially has to do with the kind of society in which we live. Our condition is such that, except for a lucky few of us, no sober education is available to us and the lives of the great masses of people are lives which are very bleak indeed and, to add to the horror of it, unnecessarily so. That, in such circumstances, nostrums abound is hardly surprising.

NOTES

1. John Locke, *Letter Concerning Toleration.* Quoted by David Gauthier in his "Why Ought One Obey God? Reflections on Hobbes and Locke," *Canadian Journal of Philosophy* 7, no. 3 (September 1977): 425.
2. Ibid., pp. 425-26.
3. See chapters 2 and 3 of this volume.
4. J. N. Findlay, "The Justification of Attitudes" in his *Language, Mind and Value* (London: Allen & Unwin, 1963).
5. Kai Nielsen, "On the Rationality of Groundless Believing," *Idealistic Studies* 11, no. 3 (September 1981): 217-29.
6. David Gauthier, "Bargaining Our Way Into Morality," *Philosophic Exchange* 2, no. 5 (Summer 1979): 15-27 and Kurt Baier, "Meaning and Morals" in Paul Kurtz (ed.), *Moral Problems in Contemporary Society* (Englewood Cliffs, New Jersey: Prentice-Hall Inc., 1969), pp. 33-47.
7. Baier, "Meaning and Morals". This essay should be supplemented by a study of a cluster of Baier's related recent articles. See the following: "The Social Source of Reason," *Proceedings and Addresses of the American Philosophical Association* 51 (1978); "Moral Reasons and Reasons to be Moral" in A. I. Goldman and J. Kim (eds.), *Values and Morals* (Dordrecht: Reidel, 1978); "Defining Morality Without Prejudice", *The Monist* 64 (1981); "Moral Reasons," *Midwest Studies in Philosophy* 3 (1978); and "The Conceptual Link Between Morality and Rationality," *Nous* 26, no. 1 (March 1982).
8. Baier, "Meaning and Morals," p. 46.
9. Ibid. See also Kurt Baier, "Moral Obligations," *American Philosophical Quarterly* 3, no. 3 (July 1966).
10. Ibid., p. 40.
11. Ibid.
12. Ibid.
13. Ibid.
14. Ibid.
15. Ibid.
16. Ibid., p. 41.
17. Ibid., p. 42.
18. Ibid.
19. Ibid.
20. Ibid.
21. Ibid., p. 43.
22. Ibid.
23. Ibid.
24. Ibid., p. 25.
25. Ibid.
26. Ibid.
27. Ibid., p. 46.
28. Ibid.
29. Baier attempts rigorously to demonstrate this in his "The Conceptual Link Between Morality and Rationality," *Nous* 16, no. 1 (March 1982): 77-78. See, in response, my "Baier on the Link Between Immorality and Irrationality," *Nous* 16, no. 1 (March 1982): 91-92.
30. David Hume, *Enquiry into Morals,* Section II, Pt. III.
31. Ibid.

32. Ibid.

33. David Gauthier, "David Hume, Contractarian," *The Philosophical Review* 88, no. 1 (January 1979): 26.

34. Ibid., p. 28.

35. Ruth Macklin, "Moral Progress," *Ethics* 87, no. 3 (July 1977): 377.

36. See my "On Needing a Moral Theory," *Metaphilosophy* (1982) and my "Grounding Rights and a Method of Reflective Equilibrium," *Inquiry* (1982).

8

Death and the Meaning of Life

I

For intellectuals, at least, the effects of the posture of modernity is very pervasive. It characteristically leaves us with a fear of being caught out in trivialities and with a fear of saying the obvious.[1] This leads us to indirect discourse, to a penchant for being clever and, because of that very fear of saying the obvious, into triviality. Certainly on a topic such as our present one such anxieties readily surface and no doubt have a reasonable object. However, without any posturing at all, I shall simply brush them aside and plunge into my subject.

Most of what I say here I have said before and it has, as well, been said before by many others.[2] Moreover, it is my belief that most of the claims made here should be a series of commonplaces, but, given the direction of our popular culture, they are not. I repeat them because they seem to me to be true, to be truths that are repeatedly avoided and that need to be taken to heart.

J. M. Cameron, a distinguished Roman Catholic philosopher whose work I admire, has remarked that more and more people today think "that to die is to be annihilated."[3] Particularly

Originally published in *The Search for Values in a Changing World* (New York: International Culture Foundation, 1978), pp. 89–102.

184

for very many of us who are intellectuals and are touched by modernity and the swarth of our secular culture, belief in the survival of bodily death is an impossibility. It seems to many of us at best a groundless bit of fantasy and at worst a conception that is through and through incoherent.[4] It is an interesting point, a point that I shall not pursue here, whether the philosophical arguments purporting to establish these thoroughly secular beliefs are sound or whether they simply reflect the *Weltbild*—itself without grounds—of the dominant secular culture with its deeply scientistic orientation.[5] Whatever we should say about this, it remains the case that among the intelligentsia, and to a not inconsiderable degree elsewhere as well, belief in the survival of death is either a very considerable stumbling block or something dismissed out of hand as simply "beyond belief" for anyone who can look at the world nonevasively and think tolerably clearly.

Even Cameron, who presumably does believe in some form of the survival of the death of at least our present bodies, recognizes that for most men "the hypothesis of survival" is "impossibly difficult."[6] Annihilation seems plainly and evidently to be our end. Yet he thinks that the "full terror of death" and the need to give some significance to our lives will drive us, if we are honest with ourselves and probing, to such an at least seemingly implausible belief.[7]

I want to resist this. I shall argue that, even if death is, as I believe it to be, utter annihilation, we can still find significance in our lives and that, if we will think carefully and indeed humanly—from the emotions or existentially if you will— we need not, and indeed should not, feel death to be such a stark terror. Cameron, like Kierkegaard, seems to take it as almost true by definition that to be fully human is to react to death. But why should we accept this conventional wisdom?

I shall, for a moment, as seems to me appropriate in this context, speak personally. Even though Tolstoy, Dostoevsky, and Pascal have deeply touched my life, I do not feel terror when I dwell on death. Yet I know full well it must come and I firmly believe—believe without a shadow of doubt—that it will mean my utter annihilation. Yet I am without such a dread of death, though, of course, when I think of it, I feel regret that I must die, but, unlike Ivan Ilyitch, I do not feel that "before its face" all life is meaningless: nothing is worth experiencing or doing. As I am now in possession of the normal powers of life, with things I want to do and experience, with pleasure in life and with people I very much care for and who care for me, I certainly do not want to die. I should very much like, in such a state, to go on living forever. Yet plainly I cannot. In the face of this, it seems to me both a sane response and a human response to that inevitability to rather wistfully regret that fact about our common human lot and to want to make the most of the life one has. But I see no reason to make a mystery of death. And I see no reason that reflecting on my death should fill me with terror or dread or despair. One takes rational precautions against premature death and faces the rest stoically, as Freud did and as Samuel Johnson came to, and as I am confident countless others have as well. Death should only be dreadful if one's life has been a waste.

By a conventionalist's sulk such an attitude, as I have just evinced, is thought to be a shallow one devoid of the depth and the *angst* that Cameron evinces or that he finds in Ernest Becker's *The Denial of Death* or that we find in the existentialists. (I do not speak here of Nietzsche.) John Austin, when he was dying of cancer and knew that he was dying of cancer but others did not, was reported to have responded to a talk by Gabriel Marcel on death by remarking "Professor Marcel, we all know we have to die, but why do we have to sing songs about it?" The conventional wisdom would make this a shallow response, but, coupled with an understanding of the integrity and importance of Austin's work and with a knowledge of Austin's fierce determination to work right up to the end, it seems to me to be just the opposite. We know we must die; we would rather not, but why must we suffer *angst,* engage in theatrics, and create myths for ourselves. Why not simply face it and get on with the living of our lives?

II

There is a tradition, finding its most persistent expression in Christianity, which contends that without life everlasting, without some survival of the death of one's present body and without the reality of God to ensure that such a life will have a certain character, life will be pointless and morality without significance. I shall now argue that these beliefs, common as they are, are not true.

It is indeed true that moral perplexity runs deep and moral ambivalence and anguish should be extensive. A recognition of this should be common ground between morally sensitive believers and skeptics. But there is no need to have the religious commitments of Christianity or its sister religions or any religious commitment at all to make sense of morality. Torturing human beings is vile; exploiting and degrading human beings is through-and-through evil; cruelty to human beings and animals is, morally speaking, unacceptable; and treating one's promises lightly or being careless about the truth is wrong. If we know anything to be wrong, we know these things to be wrong and they would be wrong and just as wrong in a Godless world and in a world in which personal annihilation is inevitable as in a world with God and in which there is eternal life.

There is indeed a philosophical problem about how we know these things to be wrong, but this is as much a problem for the believer as for the skeptic. I would say that for anyone— for believer and skeptic alike—if he or she has an understanding of what it is to take the moral point of view, he or she will, *eo ipso*, understand that it is wrong to harm others, that promises are to be kept, and the truth to be told. This does not mean that he or she will be committed to the belief that a lie *never* can rightly be told, that a promise *never* can be broken or that a human being in *no circumstances* can rightly be harmed. But, if there is no understanding that such acts always require very special justification and that the presumption of morality is always against them, then there is no understanding of the concept of morality. But this understanding is not intrinsically or logically bound up with knowing God or knowing about God or the taking of a religious point of view or knowing or even believing that one will survive the death of one's "earthly body".

It might be responded that such an understanding does imply a knowledge of the reality of God because we *only* know these things to be wrong because we know they are against God's will and something is only good because God wills it and is only wrong because God prohibits it. Leaving aside skeptical questions about how we can know, or whether we can know, what God does and does not will, the old question arises whether something is good simply because God wills it or does God will it because it is good? What is plain—leaving aside God for a moment—is that something is not good simply because it is willed or commanded; indeed it is not even morally speaking, a good thing to do simply because it is willed or commanded by an omnipotently powerful being, unless we want to reduce morality to power worship, as has one rather well known but (on this issue) confused philosopher.[8] But might—naked power—doesn't make right. And there is no implication that it will become right even when conjoined with faultless intelligence. There can be—and indeed are—thoroughly ruthless, exploitative, manipulative people who are very intelligent indeed. Neither omnipotence nor omniscience imply goodness.

However, it is still not implausible to say that it is *God's* willing it which makes all the difference, for God, after all, is the supreme, perfect good. But I in turn ask, how do we know that or do we know that? If we say we know it through studying the Scriptures and through the example of Jesus, then it should in turn be responded that it is only in virtue of our own quite independent moral understanding of the goodness of his behavior and the behavior of the characters in the Bible that we come to recognize this. Moral understanding is not grounded in a belief in God; just the reverse is the case: an understanding of the religious *significance* of Jesus and the Scriptures presupposes a moral understanding.

If, alternatively, we claim that we do not come to understand that God is the supreme and perfect good in that way but claim that it is a necessary truth—a proposition, like 'Puppies are young dogs', which is true by definition—then we still should ask: how do we understand that putatively necessary proposition? But again we should recognize that it is only by having an understanding of what goodness is that we come to have some glimmering of the more complex and extremely perplexing notions of supreme goodness or perfect goodness. The crucial thing to see is that there are things that we can recognize on reflection to be wrong, God or no God, and that we can be far more confident that we are right in claiming that they are wrong, than we can be in claiming any knowledge of God or God's order.

Finally, someone might say that since God is the cause of everything, there could be no goodness or anything else if there were no God. But this confuses *causes* and *reasons,* confuses questions about causally bringing something into existence or sustaining its existence and justifying its existence. If there is the God of the Jews and the Christians everything causally depends on Him, but still, even if there were no God who made the world, it would still be wrong to torture little children, and even if there were no people to be kind, it would be timelessly true that human kindness would be a good thing and that the goodness of human kindness does not become good or cease to become good by God's fiat or anyone else's. And it is in no way dependent on whether we live out our fourscore years and ten or whether life is everlasting.

In terms of its fundamental rationale, morality is utterly independent of belief in God or a belief in immortality. To make sense of our lives as moral beings there is no need to make what may be an intellectually stultifying blind leap of religious faith or to in any way believe in an afterlife. Such a moral understanding, as well as a capacity for moral response and action, is available to us even if we are human beings who are utterly without religious faith.

Furthermore, it does not follow that our lives are pointless, empty or meaningless if there is no God and if death is unequivocally our lot. There is no good reason to believe that because of these things we are condemned to an Oblomov-like, senseless existence. There is no reason we must despair if God is dead and if life must come to an end. If there is no God, it is indeed true that we are not blessed with the questionable blessing of being made for a purpose; furthermore, if there is neither God nor *Logos,* there is no purpose to life, no plan for the universe or providential ordering of things in accordance with which we must live our lives. Yet, from the fact, if it is a fact, that there is no purpose to life or no purposes for which we are made, it does not at all follow that there are no purposes *in* life that are worth achieving, doing, or having, so that life in reality must be just one damn thing after another that finally, senselessly terminates in death. 'Purpose of life' is ambiguous: in talking of it we can, on the one hand, be talking of 'purpose to life', or, on the other, of 'purposes in life' in the sense of plans we form, ends we seek, etc., that result from our deliberate and intentional acts and our desires, including our reflective desires. The former require something like a god or a *Logos,* but the latter most certainly do not. Yet it is only the latter that are plainly necessary to make life meaningful in the sense that there are in our lives and our environment things worthwhile doing, having, or experiencing, things that bring joy, understanding, exhilaration, or contentment to ourselves or others. That we will not have these things forever does not make them worthless any more than the inevitability of death and the probability of decay robs them, or our lives generally, of their sense. In a Godless world, in which death is inevitable, our lives are not robbed of meaning.

III

Some might concede all this and still respond that I am leaving out something crucial from the religious traditions. They could agree I have shown that life for an atheist can very well have meaning. But what I have not shown is that with the loss of the kind of hope and the kind of perspective that have gone with Judaism, Christianity, and Islam something has not been irreparably taken from us, the loss of which is increasingly felt as the managed society of the twentieth century closes in on us.

What I am alluding to can perhaps best be brought forward if I turn to a famous trio of questions of Kant's: "What can I know?" "What ought I to do?" and "What may I hope?"[9] Max Horkheimer, in commenting on them, remarks that an examination of the "third question leads to the idea of the highest good and absolute justice."[10] He then adds that the "moral conscience . . . rebels against the thought that the present state of reality is final. . . ."[11] In the struggles of our everyday life, in the world as we know it, our hopes for a realization, or even approximation, of a truly human society, a society of human brotherhood and sisterhood, a just society or even a rational society are constantly dashed, constantly defeated. This led Kant, Lessing, and even Voltaire to postulate immortality in order to make some match between our aspirations and what is realizable. Such postulations are indeed easy to satirize and indeed it is folly to try to argue from such hopes to any likelihood at all that such a reality will obtain.[12] But one can understand it as a hope—a hope that a person who truly cares about his fellows and has lost all faith in anything like a Marxist humanist future, might well keep close to his heart. If we believe, as Horkheimer and Adorno do, that we live in a world where we grow lonelier, more isolated, more caught up in meaningless work routines, more passive, more and more incapable of seeing things as a whole, and of having any believable sense of where we come from, who we are or where we are going, we may perhaps rightly become "knights of faith" and make such an otherwise absurd postulation.

Yet, if we can rightly live in hope here, can we not, even more rightly, live in accordance with the less intellectually stultifying hope that we humans can attain a certain rationality and come to see things whole and in time make real, through our struggles, a truly human society without exploitation and degradation in which all human beings will flourish? Even *if* this hope is utopian—another dream of the "dreamers of the absolute"—it is still far less utopian, and far less fantastical, than the hope for "another world" where we will go "by and by." Moreover, such secular hopes are in the various Marxisms (reified and otherwise) as alive in traditions as are the otherworldly conceptions of Christianity.

NOTES

1. The sense of this is very acute in Stanley Cavell's *Must We Mean What We Say* (New York: Charles Scribner's Sons, 1969) and this sense is further astutely conveyed in Francis Sparshott's discussion of it in *The Times Literary Supplement* (July 22, 1977): 899.
2. My *Scepticism* (London: Macmillan, 1973); "Linguistic Philosophy and 'The Meaning of Life'," *Cross-Currents* 14 (Summer 1964); "Linguistic Philosophy and Beliefs," *Philosophy Today*, No. 2, Jerry H. Gill (ed.), (London: Collier Macmillan Ltd., 1969); "An Examination of the Thomistic Theory of Natural Moral Law," *Natural Law Forum* 4 (1959); and "God and the Good: Does Morality Need Religion," *Theology Today* 21 (April 1964).
3. J. M. Cameron, "Surviving Death," *The New York Review of Books* 21, no. 17 (October 1974): 6-11.
4. Antony Flew, "Is There a Case for Disembodied Survival?" *The Journal of the American Society for Psychical Research* 66 (April 1972): 129-

44; part III of Antony Flew, *The Presumption of Atheism* (New York: Barnes & Noble, 1976); Terrence Penelhum, *Survival and Disembodied Existence* (London: Routledge & Kegan Paul, 1970); and my "Logic, Incoherence and Religion," *Sophia* 26 (October 1987): 12-21.

5. Ludwig Wittgenstein, *On Certainty*, translated by Denis Paul and G. E. M. Anscombe (Oxford: Basil Blackwell, 1969) and G. H. von Wright, "Wittgenstein on Certainty," *Problems in the Theory of Knowledge*, ed. by G. H. von Wright (The Hague: Martinus Nijhoff, 1972), pp. 47-60.

6. J. M. Cameron, op. cit., p. 11.

7. Ibid.

8. Peter Geach, *God and the Soul* (London: Routledge & Kegan Paul, 1969), pp. 117-29.

9. Immanuel Kant, *Critique of Pure Reason*, translated by J. M. D. Meiklejohn (New York: Dutton, 1934), p. 457.

10. Max Horkheimer, *Critique of Instrumental Reason* (New York: The Seabury Press, 1974), p. 2.

11. Ibid.

12. J. L. Mackie, "Sidgwick's Pessimism," *Philosophical Quarterly* (1976): 326-27.

9

Morality and the Human Situation

THE MEANING AND SOURCE OF MORALITY

Skepticism about morality is very pervasive in our society. It is itself a key element of modernism. Sometimes it is little better than a conventional posture, something that is simply accepted unreflectively by educated people as just being a part of the *Weltgeist* and an attitude of mind any knowledgeable tough-minded person would have. With others it is the result of probing and often agonizing reflection. The sources of this skepticism are varied but one very central source is what I shall call the *no-truth thesis* in ethics.[1] By this I mean the belief that over questions of fundamental values, including moral values, no question of truth or falsity can sensibly arise. That the benefits and burdens in the world are not equally distributed, is a plain matter of fact the truth of which is perfectly evident. We also have some sense of what it would be like for that claim to be false. We know, when we study some hunting and gathering societies which are approximately egalitarian, what makes that claim concerning their approximate equality true and we also have some idea of what it would be like for this to be true of the whole world. We do not, of course, expect it to be true,

From *Huamnist Ethics,* edited by Morris Storer (Buffalo, N.Y.: Prometheus Books, 1980), pp. 58-70.

but we have some idea of what it would be like for it to be true. For the moral claim that each person irrespective of merit or desert has a right to an equality of concern and respect, it is far less clear what, if anything, could show that to be true or for that matter false. Many of us feel deeply committed to some such principle even when we have no idea at all what would or could show it to be true or—if it makes any sense to talk in this way about such a principle—probably true. There can be a deep and perfectly unwavering commitment to it by people who do not believe that it or any other fundamental moral principle could be true or false. For factual claims, finally rooted in empirical observation, we understand how to determine whether they are true or false or probably true or false, but with fundamental moral claims we can have no such basis of confidence. Yet, without the possibility of ascertaining the truth or falsity of our fundamental moral commitments, it appears at least to be the case that they must rest on arbitrary decisions of principle rooted in our emotions or perhaps our biology, culture, or even class. This is one persistent and nagging source of skepticism. I shall return in a moment to considerations about how this no-truth thesis might possibly be met.

This skepticism rooted in worries about truth in ethics is exacerbated by concern about the relativity of morals. Even a rather superficial study of social anthropology will reinforce something we learn from our reading of Herodotus, namely, that moral beliefs, sometimes even very deeply embedded moral beliefs, differ widely from culture to culture and, sometimes even within a culture, cut across class. This would not be so serious a worry if we had a confident sense of truth in ethics. After all, that different tribes have different cosmologies does not make physics totter. It is when it is coupled with the no-truth thesis that cultural relativity is troublesome. With it there is reasonable worry that perhaps even our most deeply embedded and stubbornly clung to moral beliefs may be little more than the ingrained mores of our time and place. We may feel strongly about the way of life of the Ik or Dobuans, but without a coherent conception of truth in ethics we are hardly in a position to claim that one way of life is better than another. We can hardly claim, with any great confidence, that these ways of life are immoral or perhaps even irrational. What our morality is, we fear, is most fundamentally a matter of how we have been conditioned. Our moral responses are very much a matter of the heart, but what these moral emotions are is deeply affected by the culture and sometimes even by the class from which we come.

Such considerations threaten the rationality and objectivity of morals. It would be foolish to believe that there are any short or easy answers to the above challenges to the objectivity of morals. Indeed there may be no answers at all and something like what I have said above may be the truth about morals and if that is so, we had better learn to face it nonevasively.[2] However, before we acquiesce in that, given what is at stake, we would be wise to see if, without flights into the evasions of a religious ethic, we can discover any resources within a purely secular morality to meet such a challenge.

With respect to the no-truth thesis, it is first well to remember that it is over the fundamental claims of morality where it has its most obvious force. That we should have concern to protect the rights of Blacks whose rights are being denied in South Africa or that we should fight poverty and degrading working conditions at home can easily be shown to be true once we accept a fundamental moral principle such as the claim that each person irrespective of merit or desert has a right to an equality of concern and respect. We know something about the conditions under which such equality is possible and we know something about what undermines self-respect. Poverty, no work, certain kinds of working conditions, and racial assault do just that, so if we accept such a fundamental moral principle we can easily establish the truth of lower-level moral principles. And, as the pragmatists were fond of stressing, it is those principles, rather than the fundamental ones, which repeatedly come into play in moral argument.[3] Moreover, once this distinction is kept in mind, it is no longer so clear that science and ethics are, after all, so different in this respect. We should not forget that it is not altogether clear how we would establish the truth or falsity of the fundamental principles of science either.

Be that as it may, there is still the haunting suspicion that if we press real moral disputes sufficiently, we will quite naturally get to a moral terrain where conflicting fundamental moral principles will be brought into play. Our "moral truths" will all be dependent on them and they will conflict and we will have no idea of how their truth or falsity is to be established. Even when we agree on the facts we will find such disputes intractable, since, for such deeply embedded moral beliefs, the no-truth thesis applies.

Perhaps the plausibility of the no-truth thesis rests on a bad model of truth. Perhaps what fuels it is a correspondence model; for example, the statement 'The cat is on the mat' is true if and only if the cat is on the mat. But there is plainly truth in mathematics and the correspondence model does not work there. Perhaps that model is also entirely inappropriate in ethics and another more realistic model should replace it.

We could say that a moral claim or principle is true if it is required by the moral point of view.[4] This, of course, raises a host of questions of which probably the most obvious is, How do we determine what is the moral point of view—and indeed, is there something appropriately called the moral point of view that reason requires us to accept? Perhaps there are just different, largely culturally determined moral points of view extant in various cultures and perhaps there is no such point of view that a through and through reasonable and well-informed person must just accept to continue to be accurately so described.

Suppose, in trying to ascertain if there really is such an objective moral point of view which could determine truth in ethics, we ask why a society, any society, the Ik included, requires a moral code, any moral code at all. I think the answer is that in a world in which there are conflicting desires and interests and in a world where all people, including the dominating classes, are to one or another degree vulnerable, we need a device wider than the law for adjudicating those conflicting desires and interests that would be acceptable to all the parties involved were they to stand in positions of equality. Morality, no doubt, has many functions but this is a function it will have in all societies. In class societies such as our own where the ruling ideas are largely in the hands of the ruling class, and reflect their interests, this function will have a large overlay of moral ideology. That is to say, the dominating class will have a certain conception of what will constitute a fair adjudication of conflicts of interests. Moreover, with their control of the mass media and education, they will sell the dominated classes a certain conception of what is possible and what is an equitable adjudication of conflicts of interests. They will create a moral ideology that, if the legitimization function of the state is working well, will bamboozle them into believing that they must keep the social contract. But this is the compliment that vice pays to virtue. Such moral ideology is parasitic on a nonideological conception of morality and the moral point of view. An indispensable function of morality is to adjudicate between conflicting interests in an equitable way. The sense of 'equitable' would be given by what rational human beings would agree mutually to accept when they understood the causes of their various desires and the consequences of getting what they want. To achieve fairness in adjudication they would have to agree to the equal consideration of the interests of everyone. As both Kant and Sidgwick in effect show us, the very idea of a morality conceptually requires a commitment to fairness. There are indeed 'class moralities' but they can only rest on intellectual confusions and false consciousness. There can indeed be classist amoralists who self-consciously promote the interests of their own class and dominate the weaker classes by moral ideology and, where that does not work, by force. But this is not a moral point of view, but an amoral one parading as a morality.[5]

To take the moral point of view requires the equitable or fair adjudicating of interests. This comes, I believe, to adjudicating conflicting desires and interests so that everyone can have as much of what he or she wants as possible, compatible with others being treated in the same manner when their wants and desires to be so treated are what they would be if those people having the desires were fully informed, had carefully reflected on this information, and had taken it to heart. In many respects it would be better to cash in the fair adjudication of conflicting desires and interests simply in terms of interests and needs. Perhaps some day, when we have a more adequate account of needs and their proper scheduling, we should do just that. The worry about wants and preferences is that in class societies they are subject to ideological deformation. This impediment can only be removed practically through political action. But the theoretical conditions I placed on the relevant appeal to desires indicate in skeletal form the kind of desires that would not be ideologically manipulated desires. Perhaps such desires would also match with what human beings genuinely need or with what is in their interests.

With such a spelling out of the moral point of view, we could then determine what in the way of rules and principles the moral point of view requires and the ones they require would be our central moral truths. The *prima facie* obligations to tell the truth, to keep our promises, to be benevolent, and care for our children would plainly be such truths. Even the fundamental principle of equal concern and respect, which I stated at the outset, would be a reasonable candidate for a true moral claim. With this conception and with a knowledge of how societies actually function and of the conditions of particular societies, we would have a yardstick, if not an Archimedean point, for assessing societies and ways of life and we would have grounds for not believing that morality was simply a matter of the differing mores of diverse societies.

HUMANKIND AND NATURE:
FREE WILL AND RESPONSIBILITY

None of the above can be obtained if human beings are not capable of responding as rational beings. If Dostoevsky's underground man is humankind in microcosm, no rational humanistic morality is possible. But, while Freud has taught us to recognize that our capacity for irrationality is far greater than untutored common sense would suspect, it is still not the case that we are all through-and-through irrationalists incapable of reflective self-direction. Rationality, like neurosis, is something that admits of degrees. However, we can characterize what it is, ideally, to be a thoroughly rational person or, as I would prefer to say, a reasonable human being. Of course, none of us satisfy these conditions fully—a fully reasonable person is an *ideal* type—but we can approximate these conditions in varying degrees, and in optimal social conditions (conditions such as could be had if a socialist humanism found a stable exemplification) far more of us could achieve far more of that reasonability than we presently do. Abstractly conceived, a fully rational human being is a human being who takes the most efficient means to achieve those ends he most wants; who is capable of postponement of want satisfaction when it will contribute more fully to the ensemble of his wants; who will, in the appropriate circumstances, reflectively and critically inspect his desires and aims; and who, aware of the extent of a socially imposed consciousness, sees through the ideologies and myths of his society and is aware of, and in control of, the distorting effects of his own distinctive psychological history. He will be a person capable of impartiality and fairness and will not in some fanatical or clever silly way be tied to his own hobby horses. He will be, for his time and place, an informed human being capable of acting in accordance with an accurate grasp of that information. With reasonable success, he will strive to achieve consistency and coherence in his beliefs and he will not, where he is in a cultural situation capable of combating them in the normal course of education, be held captive by irrational cosmologies such as those of Judaism and Christianity.[6] (This does not mean that a reasonable person cannot be a Christian, but it does mean a fully reasonable person in a society such as ours who has had the benefit of a sober and full education—plenty of anthropology, philosophy, and natural science—cannot be a Christian.)

Determinism is a difficult, if not impossible, thesis to prove and it indeed may not be true or even perhaps coherent. But it does appear at least to be both coherent and true or, at the very least, it appears to be something we find very difficult not to assume. My point is that in thinking in a fundamental way about morality it is not essential to prove its truth or probable truth, for as Hobbes and Hume argued, even if it is true, there is still a perfectly straightforward sense in which human beings can be both free and morally responsible moral agents. Freedom and responsibility, like reasonability, admit of degrees. It is often the case that a human being has the ability and the opportunity to do certain things. A human being is free when he has the ability and the opportunity to do such things and in those circumstances does what he wants. The hallmark of a free human being is a human being who is capable of self-direction and who actually exists in such social conditions that his behavior is self-directed rather than being compelled or constrained, either externally or more subtly by psychological forces, so that he or she lacks the ability or the opportunity to do what she or he wants to do. The opposite of human freedom is not determinism but compulsion or coercion. Even in a completely determined world there are some people in some circumstances who are able to do what they want to do when they want to do it. These people in those respects are free. To the extent that one lacks the ability or opportunity to do what one wants to do, one is unfree. This is invariably a matter of degree but the degree is all important. There are indeed certain Brave New World situations in which we could do what we want and still not be free, that is, self-directed individuals. But when the person is rational and is able to do what she wants to do, then she is free. Freedom and responsibility are crucially cashed in both in terms of being rational and being able to do what one wants to do. But both of those things are quite possible even in a fully determined world.[7]

To talk of taking the moral point of view plainly presupposes that people can be free and responsible agents. But this agency is perfectly possible and indeed is, with a not inconsiderable number of people, in varying degrees actual. In a truly human society it would be even a far more extensive social reality. Determinism does not defeat morality and there is no good reason to believe that we are such irrationalists as to make morality a Holmesless Watson.

MORALITY AS WORKABILITY
VERSUS MORALITY AS JUSTICE

Surely the mere fact that some social arrangement works does not make it right. If Hitler could have succeeded in capturing all the world and destroying all the Jews, his social system would still be quite accurately described as bestial. That it worked would not make it one jot less bestial. And if South Africa holds out—or becomes a model for the world—and shows its social system to be more efficient and to create more capital accumulation than any alternative system, it still would remain a moral monstrosity. Efficiency and workability is more important in a political morality than is generally recognized. But it is not the whole of such a morality and Pareto optimality can be outweighed by other considerations.

From our characterization of the moral point of view, it is a conceptual requirement that, morally speaking, the interests of everyone be considered alike. This means that restrictions are put on a utilitarian determination of desirable ends. We must not only seek the maximizing of happiness or whatever else is taken to be intrinsically good, we must also seek a maximization constrained by a certain pattern of distribution. There are questions of individual justice that are a matter of entitlement, but social justice is largely concerned with patterns of distribution of the benefits and burdens of a society. Once a certain threshold of scarcity is passed—a threshold long since passed in the Western Democracies—what is the right thing to do is not determined simply by what will produce the greatest aggregate of intrinsic good. Situations could arise where the moral point of view would require opting for a slightly lesser total of intrinsic good more equitably distributed.

The equitable distribution I would defend is egalitarian. It seems to me that the principles of social justice that should govern the design of an affluent society are the following:

1. Each person is to have an equal right to the most extensive total system of equal basic liberties and opportunities (including equal opportunities for meaningful work, for self-determination and political participation) compatible with a similar treatment of all. (This principle gives expression to a commitment to attain and/or sustain equal moral autonomy and equal self-respect.)

2. After provisions are made for common social (community) values, for capital overhead to preserve the society's productive capacity, and allowances are made for differing unmanipulated needs and preferences, the income and wealth (the common stock of means) is to be so divided that each person will have a right to an equal share. The necessary burdens requisite to enhance well-being are also to be equally shared, subject, of course, to limitations by differing abilities and differing situations (natural environment, not class position).

My first principle is like Rawls's in being an equal liberty principle. The stress here is on the importance for everyone of moral autonomy and an equality of self-respect. The crucial thing about that first principle is its insistence that in a through-and-through just society we must all, if we are not children, mentally defective, or senile, be in a position to control the design of our own lives and that we must in our collective decisions have a right to an equal say. Where conditions of relative abundance obtain (conditions similar to those in Japan, most of North America, and much of Europe) equal self-respect and moral autonomy require something like my second principle to be attainable. Without something like my second principle, disparities in power and authority, acceptable under a less egalitarian system, indeed even under a system as egalitarian as Rawls's, will undermine the self-respect of people on the lower rungs of that less egalitarian society. Once we have achieved relative abundance, a greater equality of self-respect and a more secure moral autonomy become preferable from a moral point of view to more goodies. (Skeptical query: Is this so for any through-and-through rational person or only for such a person if he also has a distinctive sense of justice?) Where one is in dire poverty one may not attach so much importance to such values but as one gains a certain threshold of economic security—attains conditions of moderate scarcity or relative abundance—effective control over one's life tends to gain in importance. If people act in accordance with my second principle, there will be a reduction of inequalities in primary goods—goods that are the source of distinctions that will give one person power or control over another. What is morally important to recognize is that status distinctions should be viewed with suspicion. A world of master and servant, boss and bossed, is not a world in which the principles of justice have received their most adequate exemplification. Justice requires that everyone should be treated equally as moral persons and, in spite of what will often be rather different conduct, everyone should be viewed as having equal moral worth. Justice in society as a whole ought to be understood as requiring that each person be treated with equal respect irrespective of desert and that each person be entitled to self-respect irrespective of desert.

THE BASIS OF RIGHTS AND DUTIES

The egalitarian principles of justice I articulated in the previous section determine the conception of rights I would defend. Given such a conception of justice, there must be certain human rights that any person simply and unforfeitably possesses just in virtue of being a human being. People are, as a matter of fact, in important ways unequal. We are not all equally caring where others are concerned or for that matter even for ourselves; we vary not inconsiderably in our moral sensitivity, in our industry, in our perseverance, in our intelligence, in our courage, in our capacity for love, and in the development of our sense of justice. It is to be hoped and indeed expected that in a social environment that is changed in certain distinctive ways these differences, though not all differences, between human beings would be considerably lessened. But be that as it may, no doubt differences would remain. With the principles of justice I have articulated, there would be a fundamental respect in which those differences would be overlooked. Justice is not determined by desert. The morality I would defend commits me to a principle of equal respect for all human beings. Human beings, great and small, good and bad, deserving and undeserving, have a right to our equal concern for their well-being and self-respect. This, I take it, is what it means to say that persons must be equally respected. This does not mean that human beings are never to receive rewards or praise or have our respect for their various accomplishments and it does not mean that certain people cannot be rightly punished or deprived of certain liberties to keep them from harming others and even, under certain extreme circumstances, from harming themselves. What it does mean is that any human being, even someone who is vicious and untrustworthy, cannot be so treated that his vital interests are simply ignored, simply set aside as counting for nothing. We do well to protect ourselves against him, but in our deliberations about what to do, his vital interests, as ours, count and count equally.

The rights we have flow from what we consider to be our vital interests. What exactly they are will be a matter of dispute and one way of marking the differences between conservatives, liberals, and socialists is to see how wide a scope they give to what they take to be the vital interests and thus the human rights of all human beings: the things a human being will have a *prima facie* right to simply in virtue of being human. These include such human rights as security of person; freedom from arbitrary arrest; the right to the means of life (food, shelter, clothing, health care); the right to work, to marry, to immigrate, to freedom of speech, to assembly, and to political self-determination. There will, of course, be a dispute about what exactly goes on the list and about the extent and nature of the heterogeneity of types of rights on the list, but all of the above, I would argue, must go on the list, for they are necessary to protect two very fundamental goods essential for sustaining the moral point of view, namely, human autonomy and the good of self-respect. Where these rights are not in force, such fundamental human goods cannot be sustained or at least maximally sustained.

These human rights cannot be forfeited, but since these rights, as all rights, are *prima facie*, they can be overridden. They cannot, however, be rightly overridden when overriding them would only provide, everything considered, some small utilitarian gain.[8] Thus, if we can show that in society C for a given time (say a decade) a marginal overall benefit would obtain by overriding the right to freedom of association and choice of domicile of a small minority M, this would not justify a denial of such rights. But during a catastrophic war where there was, in reality and not just in an inflamed popular imagination, a clear and present danger that would bring catastrophic harm to the society and perhaps suffering and death for a very large percentage of that society, then in such a circumstance one would, if there is no other way of preventing it, be justified in· overriding such rights to prevent a catastrophe. It is not that the rights are forfeited, for they can't be, but they are overridden, and rightly, to prevent some still greater evil.[9] But they cannot be justifiably overridden, as utilitarians suppose, simply by showing that some greater maximizing of overall utilities would obtain by overriding them.

People can have rights without corresponding duties or obligations. Infants, the enfeebled, and perhaps even some animals have rights without having duties and obligations and in any case the correlation does not apply universally, but many rights do carry with them duties and obligations. If you have the right to freedom of speech or assembly, I have a duty not to try to prevent you from doing these things, and it is the obligation of the state authorities to provide a social situation in which these rights can be exercised.

PRINCIPLES IN SITUATIONAL MORALITY

If my argument has been near to the mark, morality is not totally situational. And it is not (what is not quite the same thing) simply a matter of the mores of one's tribe or of what one just happens to like or approve. There can be true or false moral claims, an intersubjective validity to moral claims, and a rationale to a morality rooted in an underlying function of morality that in turn determines what it is to take the moral point of view. People have objective interests and genuine needs.[10] But not everyone's needs can always be satisfied and not all interests are compatible. It is a pervasive function of morality to adjudicate these conflicts in a fair way, but neither what constitutes a "fair way" nor what are the interests and needs of human beings can be determined purely situationally. There are needs and interests that are quite universal, such as the need for companionship, some privacy, security, and some meaningful work. They have, of course, a cultural overlay. Neither privacy nor meaningful work will have quite the same meaning for a Samoan as it will for a Swede. Thus, there must be a certain specific situational determination, but there are common features too and general parameters set by interests and needs which are quite pan human. Again fidelity between husband and wife will not be the same for a Samoan as for a Sicilian, and for a Swede it will still be something different again and within a given culture this will change over time. Still there are bonds of trust, getting different cultural phrasings and applying differently in different environments and different social structures, which will have a very similar rationale. This similar rationale is what gives sense to the very concept of fidelity. Because such key concepts in our lives have such underlying rationales, the actions of quite different peoples are intelligible to one another. The truth about situationalism is that there are many moral conceptions such as certain marriage relationships or certain property rights which only make sense in a determinate social setting. In short, the environment, both physical and social, sets limits to the appropriateness of moral actions. The treatment of the aged by aboriginal Tasmanians makes moral sense. But it would be vile in contemporary Tennessee. The cattle raiding of the Turkana, Nuer, and Dinka makes sense and perhaps is, everything considered, justifiable. Cattle rustling in Texas and Alberta is another thing again. But this kind of situationalism is neither relativism nor opportunism. The differences are best explained in terms of different applications of noncontextual general moral principles. We have culture—specific moral practices that make perfectly good sense in terms of general moral principles just as different conventions about what side of the road to drive on make sense in terms of an overall conception of safe driving. And just as there can be a coherent dispute about which states or provinces have the most adequate driving regulations, so there can be an assessment, often mistaken and sometimes ethnocentric, but not necessarily either, of the moral practices and the overall moral code of different cultures in terms of what the moral code requires and a reasonable assessment of the facts in the case.

Perhaps in some sense morality is an expression of the whims of mortal will, but if so, it is a rational will, and it includes the possibility, and indeed the virtual certainty, that many such wills will be mistaken and that their very mistakes can be corrected from within the unfettering confines of a rational conception of the moral point of view. It is not the case that morality is simply a matter of the heart, though it is that too, and it is not a matter of "you pays your money and you takes your choice" in which decision and simple desire is king. What is good is determined by what answers to human interests, what satisfies human needs, and what furthers human self-realization. But morality is not simply what is in a person's interest, the interest of a ruling class, what is desired by an agent or approved of in his tribe. Kant and Sidgwick were far too rationalistic in thinking that morality is a "dictate of reason" but all the same it is none of the above-mentioned things and it is not an irrational escape in an absurd world not of our making.

NOTES

1. See my "On Deriving an Ought from an Is," *The Review of Metaphysics* 32, no. 3 (March 1979).

2. There can, of course, be truths *about* morals even if there are no moral truths. He who would raise fat geese need not himself be fat.

3. John Dewey, *The Quest For Certainty* (New York: G. P. Putnam's Sons, 1929). But perhaps even more fully Dewey's views on ethics, relevant to the above claim, come out in the excellent collection of his work in John Dewey, *Intelligence in the Modern World* (New York: The Modern Library, 1939), pp. 761-93. However, the best statement of this pragmatist view—a statement fully cognizant of the critical reactions to it—is to be found in Sidney Hook, *The Quest for Being* (New York: St. Martin's Press, 1961), pp. 49-70.

4. Kurt Baier, *The Moral Point of View* (Ithaca, New York: Cornell University Press, 1958) and Kai Nielsen, "On Moral Truth" in Nicholas Rescher (ed.) *Studies in Moral Philosophy* (Oxford, England: Basil Blackwell's Ltd., 1968). This account has been powerfully criticized by James R. Flynn, "The Realm of the Moral," *American Philosophical Quarterly* 13, no. 4 (October 1976). I try, in the present essay, to state my account in such a way so as not to be vulnerable to those criticisms.

5. See my "Rawls and Classist Amoralism," *Mind* (January 1977) and my "Morality and Classist Amoralism," *Philosophical Studies* (The National University of Ireland, 1979).

6. What I have said about rationality is cryptically expressed here. I have developed it in my "Principles of Rationality," *Philosophical Papers* 3, no. 2 (October 1974); "The Embeddedness of Conceptual Relativism," *Dialogos* 11, no. 29-30 (November 1977); and my "Rationality, Needs and Politics," *Cultural Hermeneutics* 4 (1977).

7. The topic of freedom, determinism and moral responsibility is an incredibly complicated one. I have, in what is perhaps an overly simple way, tried to hack through some of those complexities. For a fuller treatment see my *Reason and Practice* (New York: Harper and Row, 1971), Part One. Sidney Hook cuts through that tangle in an even brusker way in his *Quest for Being*, pp. 26-48. But it seems to me that what he says there is essentially sound.

8. This is powerfully argued by Ronald Dworkin in his *Taking Rights Seriously*, (Cambridge, Massachusetts: Harvard University Press, 1977).

9. Joel Feinberg, "The Nature and Value of Rights," in *Rights*, David Lyons (ed.) (Belmont, California: Wadsworth Publishing Company, Inc., 1978), pp. 78-91.

10. For some important discussions of needs see Ross Fitzgerald (ed.), *Human Needs and Politics* (Oxford, England: Pergamon Press, 1977) and William Leiss, *The Limits of Satisfaction* (Toronto, Ontario: The University of Toronto Press, 1976).

9975